MAXIMUM MOMENTUM

HOW TO GET IT, HOW TO KEEP IT.

MIKE BERLAND

with Lauren W. Morgan

Regan Arts.

This book is dedicated to all of those who
Decode data into Momentum at Decode_M.

Regan Arts.

First Regan Arts paperback edition, March 2020

Library of Congress Control Number: 2019954918

ISBN 978-1-68245-126-7

Book design by Aubrey Khan, Neuwirth & Associates
Cover by Alisha Petro

Printed in the United States

CONTENTS

MOMENTUM

A New Vocabulary...

Pay attention to these words:

Mass . . . Velocity . . . Acceleration . . .
Energy . . . Drive . . . Thrust . . .

Can you feel the lift in your chest?

Now, consider these words:

Stagnation . . . Complacency . . .
Torpor . . . Apathy . . .

Do you feel a slump?

This is the vocabulary of momentum.

In the coming pages, you'll become immersed in this new vocabulary, internalizing the cornerstone of potential and the science behind it. You'll never see success the same way again.

And your best days will always be ahead of you.

ACKNOWLEDGMENTS

Let's go back to physics. Momentum doesn't start without an object. There has to be something that exists in the beginning, which, when it's impacted by forces, starts to move. For us, the object was the idea that momentum could be quantified in communications and that would explain cultural relevancy—brands, politicians, movements, culture, celebrities, and even personal growth.

We knew that the world was changing. In our current era, the old systems of communications and brand metrics no longer worked, or were not applicable. So, like all good scientists, we went into the lab to study the matter. Quantifying momentum was no easy task. And like all lab efforts, it took years.

In any lab, there is a team of researchers who play different roles, all essential to the ultimate success of the effort. Our lab had an eclectic group of scientists, strategists, and mathematicians. We even had a provocateur. We were all convinced that momentum could be quantified, and this knowledge would provide a breakthrough in communications and beyond.

This book demonstrates the effectiveness of our investigation.

Like all good scientific journals, I want to give full credit to the team:

Lauren Morgan always kept me honest and grounded—making sure my ideas worked in the real world. She was the steady, committed presence who held the team together.

Kevin McSpadden was our chief provocateur, who gave us the confidence that momentum mattered in today's world.

Micah Wilson kept us real by reminding us of high school physics and Sir Isaac Newton's formula that Momentum = Mass x Velocity.

Brendan Downing and Jo Denby gave velocity to our momentum effort.

Success in the lab is only part of the success of any project. Being able to communicate it to the outside world is just as important. Catherine Whitney's enthusiasm, passion, and commitment to telling our story accelerated our momentum exponentially. Her style, insight, and deep understanding allowed us to bring the theory, formulas, and examples together with a deft touch. Her best days are certainly bright and shining ahead.

And then there is Meredith Keller, who kept all of our momentum moving forward. Anyone who is familiar with forces knows that her role was the hardest task of all.

Every lab needs a sponsor. I am especially grateful to Judith Regan, the visionary who saw the potential of my work and supported this project from the beginning. Judith's genius is the ability to both recognize and create momentum, and her confidence and spirit were constants.

Our editor, Mitchell Jackson, was patient, thorough, and insightful—always ready with a smart solution when we got stuck. He lived the process with us.

INTRODUCTION

My Best Days Are Ahead

Are your best days ahead of or behind you?

It is an interesting question to ask.

It is an easy question to answer.

But it is a hard question to answer *truthfully*.

Most people feel entitled to have their best days ahead. And then they wonder what went wrong when they discover that it isn't so. What happened? Who can they blame?

We're left to wonder: How do some people always seem to be in the right place at the right time? Is it luck—or something else?

Assessing the question "Are my best days ahead or behind?" is a key component of the study of momentum.

It has been a way of life for me. It's reflected in:

- Every decision I make.
- Every brand I see.
- Every town I visit.
- Every employee I hire.
- Every politician I consider.

- Every post on social media I read or write.
- Every meeting I have.
- Every race I run.

All go through the same "best days ahead" test: Is this going *somewhere?* Will it lead to something *positive?* I know one thing: I always want to be a part of whatever is in the "best days ahead" category.

People who know me know that I never say no to something that carries a sense of possibility and optimism. Even if it means overcommitting, double booking, or traveling around the world, I follow each opportunity because I never know where it will lead. If it's moving, I'm going to keep moving with it.

In the movie *Annie Hall*, Alvy Singer is having a conversation with Annie Hall, and he says: "A relationship, I think, is like a shark. You know? It has to constantly move forward, or it dies. And what we got on our hands is a dead shark."

A shark stays alive by moving forward. It has to keep its momentum, or it dies. That is pretty extreme. But that's my story; I am that shark. That's not to say I am predatory. I'm just always moving forward, always maintaining momentum. For me, momentum takes constant work. It doesn't just happen, and it's definitely not easy. You have to be savvy, nimble, and one step ahead all the time. I have achieved Maximum Momentum through Momentum Milestones that have kept me moving forward. Here are some of my early ones.

MOMENTUM MILESTONE 1:
Taking Control of My Life

I know exactly when I became a shark. I know the moment that I took control of my life and affirmatively decided my best days would always be ahead.

Growing up Jewish in Chicago came with the expectation that, when you turned thirteen, you would be bar mitzvahed. It meant years of attending Hebrew school after regular school, practicing my Haftorah and Torah portions for endless hours as the date approached, and writing my first publicly delivered speech.

In Judaism, the bar mitzvah is the symbolic rite of passage of a boy becoming a man. But for me, it was greater than that, and I was determined to make my bar mitzvah much more meaningful. I decided that my bar mitzvah would signal the day when I took control of my life and started to make decisions for myself.

On May 2, 1981, I made two key decisions:

- To give myself a middle name—Jay. Nothing fancy or symbolic, but with a middle name, I would feel complete and in control. (As Michael J. Fox became a more popular actor—*Family Ties*, *Back to the Future*, etc.—I knew I had made the right decision.)
- To leave my house in the suburbs to attend the Latin School of Chicago, an academically rigorous high school in the city. That decision inspired me and prepared me for the rest of my life.

What united these two decisions was that I was taking control of my future—my name, my brain, my experience—and that led to opportunities. My momentum was starting.

And yet, both decisions came with profound consequences. Giving myself a name was rejecting a long-standing family tradition of boys not having middle names. It was a ridiculous tradition, but I got a lot of flak for bucking it. I didn't want my family to control my momentum, and this was the first way to seize it.

KEY MOMENTUM LESSONS

▸ It is never too early or too late to start. By definition, you can always start building momentum.

▸ You have to be in control of the decisions that affect you. Having independence is critical.

▸ Keeping momentum comes with consequences. People around you will be impacted.

MOMENTUM MILESTONE 2:
The Nose Knows

There were three requirements for growing up in Chicago: (1) We rooted for our sports teams with our hearts, not our heads. We adored lovable losers like the Cubs, Monsters of the Midway who didn't win Super Bowls, and hockey teams you couldn't even watch on local TV; (2) We were Democrats. Politics was a political machine controlled by one family from one part of the city—the Daleys; (3) We did what we were told or paid the consequences. People fell in line in Chicago. In those days, there was very little tolerance for new ideas.

But as I attended the Latin School for high school, the norms of Chicago were changing: the Bears and Cubs were winning; Chicago elected its first black mayor, Harold Washington; and suddenly, new ideas were everywhere.

I could feel something happening in Chicago, and I wanted to be part of it.

I was an avid fan of a popular local paper, the *Chicago Reader*—a must-read for local issues, events, and what was going on in the neighborhood. And in the *Reader*, there was a column I loved called "The Straight Dope," written by Cecil Adams. Its tagline was "Fighting ignorance since 1973."

I was inspired and motivated and decided to do my own version of "The Straight Dope" in my column for the student newspaper, *The Forum*. I intended to raise my profile, influence my community, and become relevant beyond just being one of five hundred students.

It was clear that *The Forum* needed an overhaul. It was dull, dirty, and stuck in the 1950s. My co-editor-in-chief and I requested extra funds to modernize the paper. We introduced color text to make it resemble the *Chicago Tribune*, sold some ads, and started printing color photos.

Then I launched my column "The Nose Knows" (this was pre-rhinoplasty for me), which was inspired by "The Straight Dope." It would be my platform to fight ignorance, settle scores, make jokes, and talk about issues that were important to the community and me.

Just like "The Straight Dope," "The Nose Knows" appeared in the same place in the newspaper each issue. I wanted people to be able to find it. I knew exactly what I was doing.

I was creating my brand by building a platform that I controlled with topics and issues that would be provocative and controversial.

I also had a very specific target in mind. Not only was I appealing to my peers, but I was also writing for the adults of the school—the faculty, the administration, and the parents. I wanted to expand my influence.

In one of my first columns, I wrote a funny, tongue-in-cheek article about the challenges of teenage life, schoolwork, and parents. In the article, I referred to my stepmother, portraying her as a character straight out of "Cinderella." This was my perceived reality, embellished by my teenage grievance. It wasn't particularly fair, and it definitely wasn't kind, but like most teenagers, I focused on my sense of parental injustice, and I had a clever way with words.

I very carefully chose the fairy tale of "Cinderella" to add flair to my story. In the Disney version of "Cinderella," the hero of the story is the prince who finds Cinderella, sweeps her off her feet, and takes her away from her mean stepmom. But the real hero of "Cinderella" is the Fairy Godmother, who gets Cinderella to the ball so she can meet Prince Charming. The Fairy Godmother helps Cinderella in her time of distress, transforming an ordinary pumpkin into a carriage and four of Cinderella's mice into horses for the vehicle. I admired the Fairy Godmother.

Within hours of publishing and distributing that issue of *The Forum*, we ran out of copies, and people were coming up to me congratulating me on the article. In a matter of hours, I had reached the whole community: the administration, the faculty, the parents, and the students. "The Nose Knows" became a must-read column.

I had momentum, and I would never give it up again. Momentum was my Fairy Godmother.

KEY MOMENTUM LESSONS

▶ Momentum-makers challenge the norms and conventional wisdom.

▶ Momentum often requires controversy and can be polarizing.

▶ Building momentum can be very high profile.

MOMENTUM MILESTONE 3:
King Maker, Not King

I am asked all the time how I got into the business of being a political pollster, and how I knew I wanted to be one. The answer is pretty simple—Karen Underhill.

In high school, I was active in student government and represented my class during sophomore year. The next logical step was to be Junior Class Prefect and then, ultimately, Senior Class Prefect. At the Latin School, these were important jobs. They ran the all-school assemblies each Monday, had a voice with the administration, and were the true student leaders of the school.

But there was a problem. I lost the elections. Twice. Both times to Karen.

I realized that seeking election had a significant drawback—you could lose. And when you lose, you really have nothing to show for it. In fact, when you lose an election, you are just a loser. You have lost any momentum that you may have had, and you have to start all over again.

That's when I decided that I would be a King Maker, not a king. The king can get shot, dethroned, or overruled. The

King Maker just moves on to the next king. A King Maker can have many kings, and more kings mean more momentum.

I immediately became immersed in politics. I started attending political organizing meetings and fundraisers on the north side. Unlike Barack Obama, I was on the other side working with the Republicans. The *Chicago Sun-Times* wrote a profile piece on me as not being old enough to vote (I was only sixteen), but I was old enough to organize and be a Republican precinct captain in Chicago's affluent Gold Coast neighborhood, which, at the time, was very Democratic.

I learned the ropes there. Kings depend on fact-based objective decision making. I knew my next step was to get deep into numbers. I treated college as pre-professional, and I became a pollster.

By the time I was nineteen, I was ready to expand my King Maker skills. In 1987, I moved to New York and got my start with a firm called Penn + Schoen Associates, Inc. It was one of the most important companies that no one had ever heard of. Located in a second-story walk-up on Third Avenue and 85th Street above a singularly greasy McDonald's, Mark Penn and Doug Schoen, Harvard alums and Horace Mann refugees, were defining the future with innovative systems for measuring public opinion. I wanted to be part of it. I started as an intern and didn't leave until we sold the company to WPP in 2006.

Penn + Schoen was ahead of its time. In those days, high-powered computers and software didn't exist. You had to build computers and write the software yourself. And that is precisely what Mark Penn did. He built the alpha microcomputer in his apartment in Riverdale and wrote the analytics software that allowed us to crunch millions of numbers in a matter of moments. We were able to print massive high-quality documents using a laser printer that was bigger than my apartment at the time.

There was intensity and rhythm to Penn + Schoen that made it highly addictive. As an aspiring King Maker, I was learning from two of the best: one's charm and ability to think big taught me how to inspire the king, and the other's creativity, critical thinking, and commitment to innovation taught me how to gain the king's confidence.

Penn + Schoen's speed and innovation were inspiring. There were overnight flash polls; mall tests that involved sending VHS tapes by Federal Express to malls for videos to be watched and evaluated with the results sent back overnight; an early-use neural network; and fuzzy logic. We accomplished all this while building an international network of research in eighty-three countries around the world. Penn + Schoen was ahead of its time.

Penn + Schoen had a culture of innovation, creativity, and curiosity with a no-problem-is-too-hard-to-solve mentality that would stick with me the rest of my life. At Penn + Schoen, I was starting to understand the power of *velocity*.

In 1995, I was made a partner at Penn + Schoen. At the time, the intention was to keep the name of the firm Penn + Schoen. When Penn introduced me to President Bill Clinton at an inauguration brunch before his second term, Clinton put his hand on my shoulder, looked Mark in the eyes, and said, "Mark, if Mike were your true partner, the firm would be called Penn, Schoen & Berland." I, of course, agreed with the president, and so did Mark. I immediately changed the logo from P+S to P, S & B and asked the receptionist to answer the phone, Penn, Schoen & Berland. The rest is history.

To be honest, there were a lot of quirks and idiosyncratic behavior at Penn + Schoen. For me, it was part of the charm and excitement. If you look at the Penn + Schoen alumni going back to the late eighties, it is a pretty accomplished group. It could also be controversial but wasn't afraid to rattle cages.

KEY MOMENTUM LESSONS

- ▸ Never let your ideology get in the way of your analytics. Sometimes the king gets killed.
- ▸ Momentum is enhanced by constant speed and innovation. Speed definitely comes before innovation because speed itself can be a form of innovation.
- ▸ Momentum requires an open mind to new technology and being able to unlock opportunities.
- ▸ There are a lot of quirks to momentum—quirks cause velocity.

MOMENTUM MILESTONE 4:
True Love

My true love, Marcela, rounds out my education in momentum-making. I met Marcela at Penn + Schoen, and we have been married for *twenty-eight years*. From the day I met her, I saw qualities in her that made her the perfect match for me: She is always optimistic and confident. She believes in the future and that no challenge is unattainable. She has a presence that commands any room she enters. She is smart (Fulbright scholar), beautiful, and charming.

Clearly, I married up. Most importantly, from the beginning, Marcela and I have shared goals that we achieved together. First and foremost, we wanted to be self-made. We made it a point to not accept any help along the way—we insisted on making it on our own. We craved independence and wanted to live life on our terms and not to be beholden to anyone or anything. We would do what we wanted, when we wanted, where we wanted.

We thrived on our passions. We aspired to pursue careers that would stimulate and reward us. For Marcela, that meant being a presidential campaign consultant in some of the most dangerous countries in Latin America: Venezuela, Colombia, Bolivia, Panama, and the Dominican Republic.

The most memorable call that I ever received from Marcela was on election day in Venezuela. Marcela called me on Sunday night as I was watching sports on TV. The kids weren't home. She told me that she was being chased in the streets of Caracas by the police, who were under direction from Chavez to seize her computer. Marcela had been in Caracas as an election monitor, and she had data that showed Chavez and his team had stolen the election. She was eluding the Venezuelan police by jumping from rooftop to rooftop—it sounded like something straight out of *Mission: Impossible*. When I asked her if she was okay, she said she was fine and that it was all kind of exciting. Then she said she had something important to tell me. *Hmmm* . . . I thought, waiting anxiously for tearful last words or vows of love.

Then she said that, no matter what happened to her that night, it was vital that she send her client the invoice for her trip, and she gave me an invoice and bank routing directions for her client.

All that was on Marcela's mind was getting paid. I call that true love.

•   •   •

KEY MOMENTUM LESSONS

▸ Maintaining momentum requires a partner who will be supportive and optimistic at all times.

▸ Building momentum requires a high degree of independence.

▸ Most importantly, momentum requires a value system that has a "never say no" mentality. Taking advantage, confidence, and, above all, unconditional love are paramount to momentum.

You can see where I'm going with this. I learned the power of momentum because it was there in my own life every step of the way. I carry those early lessons with me as guiding principles. I want to share the secret of momentum in every arena of life. It might surprise you.

Remember this: It's never been easier to control your momentum. It's never been easier to impact your mass and velocity. You have to speak the language and follow the science.

PART 1

THE SCIENCE OF MOMENTUM

CHAPTER ONE

THE PROPULSION FORMULA

I was sitting on the set of a TV studio in late 2015 when I started to panic. As a pollster and analyst, I was used to sharing my predictions, but in the early months of the 2016 election season, my analytics were crashing. The numbers didn't seem to matter. The percentages were useless. Predictions were futile. A new kind of candidate, Donald Trump, had surged onto the scene, and he had defied every rule of politics I knew. He was using social media like a Kardashian. He was embracing controversy while his opponents were avoiding it like the plague. He was operating like a brand more than a politician. How the hell could I measure that?

That moment was the origin of my quest to decode momentum. Suddenly, the age of polling—of analysis by the survey numbers—was over. Instead, we were living in the age of momentum as a measure of success.

In the age of momentum, the concept of "tipping points" seems almost quaint and like watching black-and-white TV or movies. When the author Malcolm Gladwell published his hit book *The Tipping Point: How Little Things Can Make a*

Big Difference in 2000, it blew people away. Everyone was enamored of tipping points as the secret catalyst to success. Just think—one little shift, one moment, one special connection, one piece of vital information could bring a slow burn to a boil, propelling a person or company or idea into the stratosphere! It was an irresistible notion.

Unfortunately, Gladwell's ideas may have been good at describing the past, but they are not relevant today. Gladwell claimed that one's ability to reach a tipping point depended on two associations—with *connectors*, people who could make the right introductions and establish the best networks; and with *mavens*, information brokers who shared their knowledge. This was an old-school way of thinking. If you're tiptoeing into a process, waiting for the "aha" moment or point of impact, you've already lost. With today's social media, we live in a world when everyone is a maven and a connector. And to turn the world upside down even more, the "traditional" media has made reporting on social media a story.

Donald Trump didn't get momentum through connections, and we know he didn't get it through information gathering. He didn't light a thousand candles; he set off a bomb. His momentum was explosive. Kylie Jenner is one of the most successful entrepreneurs of our time—all because she can go directly to her consumers. Her momentum comes because *she* is a connector and maven.

Momentum is not a slow burn that leads to a boil. Momentum is a force—you either take off or you're a dud. There is no tipping point, only constant motion.

I know why you're reading this book. You want to learn the secret of getting and keeping momentum. You might not have started as early as I did, but everybody wants momentum.

Politicians thrive on it.

Businesses and brands need it to grow.

Movements rely on it to spread their message and achieve impact.

People search for it in their personal lives.

It's a human drive to seek momentum because we want to change and transform.

But the truth is, most people think of momentum as being kind of mysterious. They credit elusive factors, like commitment, charisma, and emotion. When we watch our favorite sports team killing it on the field, we rave that the team has momentum. But why? Is it the cheering crowds that lift a team to victory? The emotional swell that allows players to perform in exceptional ways? The drive that turns one successful play into others, like a row of dominoes falling? As the proverb goes, "Nothing succeeds like success." That could be applied to sports, but it still doesn't explain momentum on the field.

There is also a misconception that when people have momentum they are lucky—they're in the right place at the right time. When you have momentum, good things happen, and your momentum gets stronger. But when you don't have momentum, or you have lost it, it seems like things get worse. Is it a matter of luck?

In the podcast "How I Built This," the host asks every guest the question, "How much of your success do you attribute to luck or just hard work?" Most of them say it's both.

An interesting fact: research shows that "lucky" people possess certain qualities that are consistent with momentum, such as optimism, openness to change, and a drive to move forward. So if they're at the right place at the right time, it's often because they chose to put themselves there.

We marvel at the come-from-behind political candidate, or the "unknown" personality who suddenly has a million followers on Twitter, or the brand that comes out of nowhere and is killing it, or an old brand that stages a comeback. What's the secret of their momentum? It can seem magical. And, just as gaining momentum feels mysterious, losing it provokes a deep sense of perplexity and angst. "What happened? Why me?" people rage, struggling to grasp how the wave they caught has crashed. Again, we think of it as emotional—people lost interest, got bored, moved on, found the next "shiny object." But again, why?

As long as we think of momentum as mysterious, we can't learn how to get it and keep it. So, let's take the mystery away and talk about physics. Momentum is actually a physics concept. Remember Sir Isaac Newton, who discovered the Law of Gravity? Newton also formulated the Laws of Motion. The Second Law states that the movement of an object is dependent on two factors: mass (size) and force (velocity). In this physics equation, momentum is mass in motion.

Let's decode that for real-life purposes. If we apply this simple calculation to politics or business or other activities in society, we can frame it this way:

Momentum =

Mass (awareness, reach, impressions, share of conversation, market share)

Velocity (excitement, polarization, virality, engagement)

To understand the difference between mass and velocity, imagine the following scenario. On your Instagram feed, you see that a band you love is going on tour next month. You like the post, and leave a comment that you're so excited they're finally coming to your city, and then head off to buy

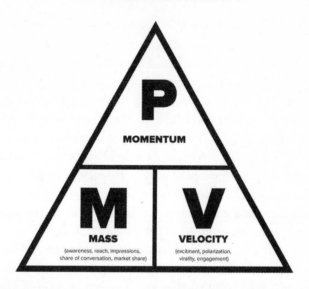

MASS	VELOCITY
FAMILIARITY: Know about it, have heard about it	**INTEREST:** Want to be a part of it
RELEVANCE: Initial interest	**INNOVATION AND CREATIVITY:** Always moving in a new direction
TRUST: Potential to become a customer or follower	**FAVORABILITY:** Popular appeal
	MISSION-DRIVEN: Appeals to people where they are

a ticket. Your engagement with their content, and excitement about seeing a band you love, contributes to their *velocity*. You've made the conversation around them a tiny bit more polarized and given a shot of energy to the next person who sees the post.

At the concert, you take a picture of you and your friends living your #bestlife and post it on Facebook. The next day, you see that your local newspaper has a brief write-up about the show in the Arts & Culture section (a *tour de force*). Both of these contribute to the band's mass, the total size of the conversation about them, across all digital and real-world channels.

Here's another example. You start seeing your friends post about a candidate they support in a local election. You've never seen them this excited about a politician before. You go to her website, and before long, you've donated to her campaign, nailed down a yard sign outside your house, and shared all of your friends' posts. The *mass* of your friends' conversation about her—the number of posts you saw in your feed—made you aware, but the *velocity* of their excitement was what pushed you over the edge to take action. Momentum can also be a self-reinforcing phenomenon— your yard sign is now part of her campaign's mass, and helps her momentum continue to build on itself.

Simply put, *mass* describes the total volume of conversation and awareness. Some mass is readily visible; sales, news articles, hashtagged posts, clicks, and some sources of mass are more abstract.

Velocity is the energy, passion, or polarization around a product, service, candidate, or issue. It points directly at emotional relevance—the question, "Does this make me feel something?"

There's a common misperception that mass is the key— the number of clicks or bodies in the room. If twenty thousand people "like" a post, that feels like momentum, especially if those likes turn into new followers. But as Hillary Clinton learned in the 2016 election, having mass (three million more votes than Donald Trump) didn't make up for the absence of velocity (excitement) in the final push. Hillary's lack of velocity gave Trump his edge.

We see this same dynamic with many brands; they leverage their initial velocity—the excitement of their new product or innovation—to grow their mass and create momentum, but then they stagnate. They don't keep moving and changing. They're too busy defending their mass and playing it safe, so it doesn't shrink. Playing it safe to protect mass ultimately has the opposite effect, because sustained momentum requires both mass and velocity.

Hillary is a study of the impotence of mass without velocity. She ran for president twice. Both times she started the campaign as the favorite, with a solid base of support in terms of voters and fundraising. In 2008, phenom Barack Obama beat her. Obama's message of hope and change had velocity. In 2016, Hillary was defeated by Donald Trump, whose Make America Great Again had velocity.

In both elections, Hillary had the mass of support to win, but her support was lackluster. No one was excited about the future with her; even the idea of the first woman president didn't spark momentum. And she was far more interested in protecting her mass than generating velocity. She'd been defending that mass through two terms as first lady (when the Lewinsky scandal actually increased her support), two terms as New York senator, and years as secretary of state. If she'd run for president against candidates with less velocity, it might have worked for her. But she had the misfortune of running against two momentum masterminds—Obama and Trump.

In short, Hillary never gained momentum. In fact, she lost momentum in both elections. Her campaigns were always on the defense, fighting to maintain support rather than moving forward. Ironically, Hillary's 2016 graphic featured a forward-pointing arrow. But her campaign never moved forward.

To have momentum, you have to keep moving and transforming. Momentum asks, "What are you going to do next . . . and can I go with you?"

In the business realm, if a lot of people buys your new product one time, you have velocity, but if they don't buy it a second time, velocity disappears. (There's a difference between a fad and momentum, which we'll explore.) Momentum is never set in stone. Without constant movement and transformation or change, momentum fizzles.

Amazon has momentum. There's no question it has mass—Amazon Prime has more than a hundred million subscribers. But it also has velocity because it is constantly changing and improvising. Jeff Bezos has said, "If you double the number of experiments you do per year, you're going to double your inventiveness."

Amazon started out selling books. Then it added other products, such as household goods, clothes, and electronics. Then it added a video streaming service. Then it added original programming. Then it added grocery shopping with the purchase of Whole Foods—with an app for two-hour delivery. The next iteration might be delivery-only grocery shopping. People might rage against Amazon for its negative impact on retail stores, but the stores weren't victims. They stagnated. They lost their momentum because they failed to innovate, and Amazon swept into the void.

I have clients that want to decode Amazon as if it could be decoded. The whole idea is that it is constantly changing. What I admire about Amazon is that it maintains its momentum by not being predictable.

Since the formula for momentum seems so obvious, why don't all companies adopt it? Why don't all political candidates pursue it? Why don't all social endeavors go for it? Why don't all brands pursue it? One answer might be a capacity for risk.

You might not think of Tide Laundry Detergent as having momentum, but the reason this brand, launched in 1946, has such staying power and remains number one is because of constant innovation, introducing stain fighters, softeners, color protection, pods, and other features—each time ahead of the market. Today it is continuing to innovate with environmentally friendly products.

Tide was able to preserve this momentum by continuous transformations, which improved its formula and benefits. Let's face it: washing clothes is still washing clothes. The washing machines may have changed, the fabrics and fashions may have changed, but Tide stays the number one brand. Why? Because it introduces innovations long before it needs to. It stays ahead of the curve by making changes while its sales are still increasing, not waiting until they're declining or a new competitor has come in. It keeps momentum by always being one step ahead.

Tide's innovations weren't easy, and they didn't just happen. Along the way, the company took a risk with every innovation. And that's the reason many don't pursue momentum: they're afraid of taking risks. *Momentum doesn't just fall into your lap.* You don't wake up one day and have momentum. To create something new and exciting, you have to go out on a limb and take a chance on the unknown. You have to do the unexpected. You have to risk failure and pick yourself up when you fall. You have to be willing to keep reinventing. Momentum takes constant work and constant change to keep moving forward.

WHAT AFFECTS VELOCITY?

Velocity is not constant. Where mass tends to expand and contract more steadily, because velocity measures the passion and intensity, it can come in volatile waves. Deftly handled, these spikes in velocity can be used to create more momentum in turn, using the media feedback cycle to your advantage. Mismanaged, they can spell disaster.

Because momentum is the product of an entity's mass and velocity, when either component doubles, momentum doubles. If their velocities were the same, you would expect McDonald's to have greater momentum than Popeye's Chicken. But if Popeye's creates so much buzz around their fried chicken sandwich that it sets the internet on fire and gets coverage from almost every national news outlet, its velocity can overtake McDonald's momentum in a heartbeat—at least for a little while. High mass gives your momentum a higher floor, but velocity will always be your ceiling.

But there is another factor—force. Force is the push or pull that is applied to an object to change its momentum. Newton's Second Law of Motion defines force as the product of *Mass x Acceleration*. Since acceleration is the change in velocity divided by time, you can connect the two concepts with the following relationship:

$$f = ma = m\frac{v}{t} = \frac{mv}{t} = \frac{p}{t}$$

Or, to put it another way:

$$p = ft$$

Momentum is force applied over time. Knowing the amount of force and the length of time that force is applied to an object will tell you the resulting change in its momentum.

What are the forces that can accelerate momentum or slow it down? Forces that can accelerate a brand are product innovations, advertising, and giveaways, or improved access and distribution. Forces that slow a brand down are company crises, malfunctions, and even changes in people's preferences—such as changing from fast food to fast-casual.

In politics, there are a multitude of ways that momentum can accelerate or slow down, and these factors can change very quickly. A stumble in a debate can slow down the momentum, just as a memorable quote can speed it up. A multitude of known or unknown factors can stall momentum—scandals, misstatements, getting caught in lies, well-positioned attacks from opponents, and so on. Savvy politicians look a few steps ahead to anticipate barriers. For example, early on, Trump began labeling the media as "Fake News," "biased," and "the enemy of the people" so that it would not be a force to slow his momentum.

Of course, nothing affects momentum in politics as much as winning or losing. That's why early primaries are so important in presidential campaigns, even though the percentage of the population is small and mostly rural (Iowa and New Hampshire). Once something has momentum, it is hard to stop, no matter which direction it's going. I think it goes to the point that momentum is usually used as a positive, but momentum for bad ideas can be hard to stop. In the same way, good ideas with momentum can get through speed bumps without an issue. Momentum gives the benefit of the doubt to good ideas, and momentum can provide strength and credibility to bad ideas.

Smaller entities need to be moving faster to have the same momentum as larger entities. If something has high mass—think of a brand like McDonald's or a politician like Joe Biden—they need less velocity than a smaller brand or politician—Chipotle or Julian Castro—to have the same momentum. But, by the same token, when high-mass entities have lost momentum, it's much harder to get them moving again. In physics, we would say that there's more inertia to be overcome before momentum can be regained. That's the reason it is easier for a startup to get momentum than a brand that has been around forever.

WHERE TO FIND VELOCITY

When we do the analysis, we're always looking for forces tied to velocity—among them innovation, future orientation, trust, emotional appeal, and loyalty. In short, we're looking for the forces that turn people into rabid fans and passionate opponents.

Best Days Ahead/Behind

- Is an industry leader vs. an industry follower
- Invented a new way of doing things
- Changes with the times vs. maintains the status quo
- Creates products/services that didn't previously exist
- Is a company that is ahead of its time
- Is making the future happen
- Changed my life for the better
- Innovates to serve customers better
- Creates time efficiency/gives me back time
- Has shown me the future
- Is a category visionary

Trust

- Has a clear mission and values
- Is transparent about its business practices
- Is transparent about its vision and where their company is going
- Delivers high-quality products and services
- Instills confidence in the company

- Is a company that customers can count on
- Provides a delightful customer experience
- Fits in with my city/community
- Is authentic to its company values
- Acts on important issues
- Is an inspiring place to work
- Communicates directly with customers/is accessible to customers
- Treats people with respect
- Puts customers first
- Does what it says it's going to do; lives up to its public commitments

Emotional Appeal

- Understands and cares about my needs
- Is relevant to my life
- Shares my values
- Has a mission that I support
- Enables me to feel connected
- Using their products and services makes me feel ethical
- Makes me feel like I'm ahead of the trend
- Makes me feel special
- Makes me feel valued
- Makes me feel heard
- Makes me feel understood
- Makes me feel that I have an impact
- Is a brand I'm proud to be associated with

Loyalty

- Is a brand I use because it's too difficult to switch to another brand
- Is a brand I can easily switch away from to a different competitive brand

- Offers a higher quality product/service than its competitors
- Offers better customer service than its competitors
- Offers a product or service better suited to my life than its competitors
- Creates interest in trying out other products/ services from the brand
- Keep buying because it has values similar to my own
- Keep buying because it gives back to communities I care about
- Has a better social media presence than its competitors
- Is a brand I keep buying from/using out of habit

FAD, TREND, OR MOMENTUM?

Momentum is different in character from trends and fads. Today, "going viral" is the trigger point of a fad. But it doesn't necessarily last. By its nature, a fad is a momentary flare of interest that dies out. A trend is more tenacious—a drift, a general direction that takes root.

Momentum can spark a trend, but it is not the same as a trend. Along the way in the development of a trend, momentum exists, but at some point, it gets absorbed into the culture and becomes "the way it is." In the mid-1980s, home computers were a rapidly developing trend. Today, they're part of the societal fabric—just there. The ubiquitous nature of Wi-Fi is a great example. Think about the trend of Wi-Fi. Dial-up, high-speed internet with a cord, then wireless internet (that you still paid for), and finally ubiquitous free Wi-Fi that you rely on and get angry if you don't have. It is not that Wi-Fi has lost its momentum. It's that it's the norm. If you don't have it, it is a problem. And you lose.

When social media began in the early 2000s, with Friendster and MySpace, it didn't show a lot of promise, seeming more of a fad—a passing fancy—than a trend. In fact, Friendster and MySpace collapsed, and later more able platforms, such as Facebook, gained momentum, followed by Twitter, Instagram, Snapchat, and others.

Early on, AOL mail was a breakthrough. Remember the movie *You've Got Mail*? It was intimate. Person-to-person. A better version of the phone. Today, AOL mail seems like a relic, but it started in motion a cascade of newer, better versions—not just email but apps, such as WhatsApp, which is now widely used, and, of course, text messaging. The point is, momentum pushes the advancement of ideas to places we never imagined they'd go, but there is always an initiator.

Social media was trending until it established itself as an integral part of technological life. It *graduated from being a trend to being the status quo, integrated into the culture*. The organic food movement gained momentum and grew from a fad into a trend over the past twenty-five years. Today it is integrated into our general food purchases. For a trend to stay status quo, it still needs momentum, or it is no longer even a thing.

But the organic universe is still reliant on innovation (and momentum!) to move it to the next level. We can see this in the *new* organic companies such as Florida Foods, which uses celery to cure chicken and bacon instead of nitrates. Their technology represents the next level of innovation.

A trend has mass, but it doesn't have velocity. Momentum, on the other hand, implies constant motion and change. A trend will ultimately lose velocity and just become the norm. Momentum gives you permission to innovate and take risks. Momentum attracts more people, more customers, more voters. It gives you a way to uncover barriers and get over them, and it allows you to contextualize and understand the competition. Without momentum, success is unreachable, and life is stagnant.

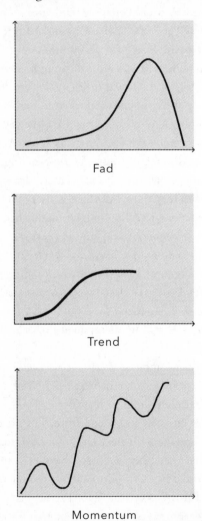

Fad

Trend

Momentum

EVERYTHING IS KNOWABLE

I will never forget the day in 2013 that I got a call from Joe B. at Facebook. It was the Friday before Memorial Day, around 3:00 p.m. I was driving up to our family home in Waccabuc, New York, for a relaxing weekend with the family.

Joe said, "We heard you have an innovative way to analyze social media conversation. We would like to meet with you next week."

At first, I thought I was getting punk'd. But I have a golden rule that I was going to apply to this situation—always say yes. You can always say no later if you have to.

So I said, "Sure, what day works next week?"

The rest is history. Facebook was the company that basically invented social media. It had the best data engineers and scientists who had written the most sophisticated algorithms to know everything about everyone but had no way to interpret what the conversations meant in the real world. They didn't understand opinions and attitudes.

What made the challenge even more exciting for me was that Facebook was interested in understanding its image and reputation. Why did people think what they thought about Facebook? At that time, they were facing issues regarding privacy and profiteering, and since young people weren't using Facebook, everyone was predicting its demise.

I spent the next year working side by side with Facebook to understand how the company ticks. I understood their business objectives and their acquisitions of Instagram and Occulus. I saw how easy they made it for people (anyone, really!) to buy targeted ads. I saw how they planned to go after the 2016 political business by giving ad buyers the ability to buy Facebook ads in specific legislative districts.

Facebook's business strategy was to try to get the advertising revenue that was going to local TV stations. It was well known that hundreds of millions of dollars were spent on politics. Facebook wanted its fair share.

Did Facebook see Fake News coming? Probably. Did they care? Absolutely not. Why? Facebook's metric was time spent on the site. Fake News is inherently interesting and gets people to engage—exactly what Facebook wanted. In 2016, Andrew Bosworth, a Facebook executive and Mark Zuckerberg confidant, wrote a memo that was later leaked, stating that negative outcomes, including terrorism and Fake News, were ultimately acceptable side effects. Facebook should stay focused on its business model, no matter what. "That's why all the work we do in growth is justified," he wrote. "All the questionable contact-importing practices. All the subtle language that helps people stay searchable by friends. All of the work we do to bring more communication in. The work we will likely have to do in China someday. All of it."

The first thing that you notice when you go to Facebook headquarters is that it is a hacker culture. (Its address is 1 Hacker Way!) At Facebook, they question authority. They believe that anything is possible, and there are no rules to play by. If you walk around, you will see posters everywhere that reinforce this notion. In fact, they developed an analog research lab that produces hacker culture videos. My favorites were: "Move Fast and Break Things," "Done Is Better than Perfect," "Proceed and Be Bold," "Fail Harder," and "Stay Focused & Keep Shipping." Posters with these slogans communicated their values and inspired their people. And they inspired me.

Let's be clear: Facebook embraced hacker culture, thriving on its place as a disrupter of the ways people got news and information. Facebook applied this goal to every facet of its business. When it became determined to be a player in the

2016 elections, it geo-coded its users into political boundaries so that politicians could target their advertising that way. Facebook became an essential part of the political landscape because now political candidates, political action committees, and virtually any other organization could target political ads without encountering the regulations that hampered their efforts in other mass communication venues. Compared to TV advertising, or direct mail through the post office, Facebook was unregulated. Its policy was to break the rules and ask for forgiveness later. It believed in the mission and felt that others didn't or would have to get there over time.

People wonder, *"Did Facebook know that its platform would be exploited?"* There is evidence that Facebook *did* know. However, it was extremely metric-driven: How much time did users stay on the site? How many people were visiting the site hourly, daily, weekly, or even monthly? That's what Facebook cared about. Politics was good for Facebook's business. Somehow, it was even more sticky than all of the photos that people were sharing. It made everyone's news feed even more sticky.

In this atmosphere, Facebook became the driving force behind Donald Trump's victory. Trump's campaign staff were adept Facebook users. One of the heads of Trump's campaign was an expert at using Facebook to sell a product, and he used that know-how to sell Trump.

Also, the Trump campaign was on the cutting edge of Facebook products. It was the Trump campaign that used Facebook Live (the service that allows live streams) to broadcast the press conference of the women supposedly assaulted by President Clinton before the second debate between Donald Trump and Hillary Clinton.

The Trump campaign realized early on that using Facebook was a much more cost-effective way to reach voters in a way that would keep moving around the site for days to come.

The most important takeaway from my work with Facebook was that everything was knowable. In the lobby of Facebook's old headquarters, there was a map of the world. On this map, lights were showing where all the users were. And you could quickly see just how ubiquitous Facebook is around the world.

Which got me to thinking, if 2.4 billion users use Facebook, consider how much data Facebook has. Think of the basics they know about Facebook users: names, birthdates, where they live, and when they use the site. Then think about the information they have, such as photos and which content engages them. This is huge.

At this moment, I concluded: Everything really is knowable; you just have to know where to look.

I had spent a career asking questions and then extrapolating and projecting the results out to populations. Now the answers were known.

Second, I had been working with the Tata Group in Mumbai and traveling to India on a fairly regular basis. I saw how ubiquitous mobile phones were. I saw the early days of the invasion of cell phone providers. I was on the cutting edge to see that mobile connectivity would be the key to improved health care, economic opportunity, etc. Maybe all the people in India weren't on smartphones, but they had text and other data capabilities.

In India and other places such as Latin America, many people in rural areas and low socioeconomic groups have cell phones with text data capabilities, but they may not be actual smartphones with internet access. These populations might not be able to afford data plans, or data plans might not be available.

Third, I bought into the idea that a connected world was a better world. I was convinced that Facebook could deliver it—I saw their commitment. Their Aquila drones would deliver the internet to those areas that didn't have it. I also saw initiatives like Google's balloon internet system. I saw the possibility of Facebook's internet.org in India that would raise smartphone penetration.

It was all very real. My thoughts about data had changed. For the majority of my career, I had believed in the power of polling. Ask questions, get answers. Analyze the data.

I understood that all the data that was needed existed in the conversations that people were already having. We could analyze the content and sentiment. Through keyword analysis, topic modeling, and automated sentiment, we could tell what was going on with consumers all over the world every second of every day.

We had all the information necessary. Maybe I was ahead of the curve, but this would be the basis of the success of Fake News.

FAKE NEWS AMERICA

If you want to know where the highest momentum was in the 2016 election, it was *Fake News*. Fake News has all the characteristics of momentum—significant mass, targeted at individual users, high velocity, and constantly changing. Not that any one piece of Fake News has momentum, but the phenomenon of Fake News is absolutely unstoppable. Regulators, politicians, and voters are naive if they think they can stop it. Never before in the history of the world has Fake News been able to spread so quickly.

People always ask me about Fake News. I have to divide my response into two parts—my ideology/beliefs and my analytics.

First of all, Fake News is nothing new. It has been around forever. Long before the *National Enquirer* appeared at every supermarket checkout, or *Pravda* became the propaganda newspaper in Russia, printing presses were spewing out newspapers, flyers, and books designed to persuade. Even before the Bible, there was Fake News.

From an analytics perspective (no judgment here), Fake News is brilliant: highly targeted, resonating headlines, graphic images, and copy that has enough of an element of truth to be believable—even though it's not true.

Fake News is so clever that it puts into question everything that is real news.

And Fake News has huge velocity and acquires mass along the way. Because it is sticky, it is shareable, and it is "a must-read."

By calling all news Fake News, President Trump has blurred the lines in a way that we may never be able to go back.

So what are the consequences of Fake News? It puts into question everything we think we know or we thought we knew. It impacts our trust. Who can we trust anymore if everything is fake?

This is perceived as a great crisis of our times, but let's stop for a moment to think about it. If Fake News has always been with us, what is different about our situation today? To be sure, the purveyors of Fake News have easier access to the masses, especially through social media. Otherwise, we're not really in a different place than we've ever been. We've always had advertising or propaganda in our midst—stuff coming at us that we have to use our brains to judge.

We say we want the TRUTH. But who decides what is true? Journalists, editors, and publications have always created news reflecting their points of view. Maybe "all the news that is fit to print" was subjective in the determination of what was fit. We have to decide.

Which all leads to a very big question: Is there morality and responsibility in momentum? The answer is a resounding yes!

Momentum can be misused or misapplied. Momentum is not always a force for good. And we have to monitor it so that it does not get out of hand. We often speak of the power of the masses or the power of the crowd. We must be careful with momentum so that it is used correctly and not misappropriated. Just remember that momentum doesn't have a moral compass. The moral compass resides with the people who consume information. One thing is clear: call it human nature or just the way the world works, but negative stories—attacks, scandals, divorces, fights—generate more momentum than positive stories. So, it's incumbent for us to be aware of what we're viewing and how we're responding. Others aren't going to do it for us. In testimony before Congress, Facebook head Mark Zuckerberg acknowledged that although candidates might lie, it wasn't Facebook's role to interfere with the public's right to hear those lies.

THE RISE OF DEEPFAKES

Going into 2020, Fake News still has momentum. It has extremely high velocity. It moves quickly because it's just intriguing enough that it could be true. People get either excited or intrigued, and they want to talk about it. It's painful, but that's our reality.

Earlier, we talked about how Facebook was a leading trigger of Fake News, which was allowed without much concern.

Fake News might change the perception of reality, but it doesn't diminish the momentum. Mark Zuckerberg has acknowledged that 126 million people were exposed to Fake News stories generated by Russian bots during the 2016 presidential campaign, and Facebook did nothing to stop them. Obviously, not everyone who saw the fake ads believed them. What if only 1 percent of people believed them? That would be 1.2 million people. What if half of the 1.2 million people were in swing states? You can see where I'm going with this.

Hillary Clinton had her negatives, as we've already described. But how much were negative attitudes based on real factors, and how much were they based on Fake News? Since the election, researchers have discovered just how much Fake News depressed Hillary's support.

A study conducted by Ohio State University researchers took people who had voted for Obama in 2012 and analyzed their reaction to three fake stories.

Here are the false stories, along with the percentages of Obama supporters who believed they were at least "probably" true:

- Clinton was in "very poor health due to a serious illness" (12 percent of Obama voters believed it).
- Pope Francis endorsed Trump (8 percent of Obama voters believed it).
- Clinton approved weapons sales to Islamic jihadists, "including ISIS" (20 percent of Obama voters believed it).

Among Obama voters who believed at least one of these Fake News stories, 45 percent voted for Clinton, while 89 percent of Obama voters who didn't believe them voted for Clinton.

Always grabbing the momentum, Trump has co-opted the term Fake News to refer to any news he doesn't like—for example, saying Russian interference in the election is Fake News. However, Fake News is a real phenomenon. And its momentum has skyrocketed with the AI development of "deepfakes."

A deepfake is a video or audio that has been engineered to look real. For example, in May 2019, a video of Speaker of the House Nancy Pelosi appeared on social media, in which she looked drunk and was slurring her words. Trump even retweeted it, expressing his condemnation. An alarmed Congress held hearings on the threat of deepfakes, but the truth is no one is sure what to do about them. Artificial intelligence has too much momentum as an uncontrolled force.

Technology can create momentum for things that aren't true. It doesn't even have to be a sophisticated effort. Amateur tinkering created a deceptive video of CNN correspondent Jim Acosta, showing him attacking a White House staffer who tried to take his microphone away during a press conference. The question is, which is stickier: the fake video or the later revelation that it had been doctored?

In a dramatic example of just deserts, Mark Zuckerberg was the victim of a fake video on Instagram, where he appeared to be boasting about his power to steal data from billions of people and control their lives.

We can hope deepfakes lose momentum, but we'll likely see even more of them in the 2020 campaign. If the campaign landscape were to be flooded by videos of candidates saying and doing outrageous things, the dizzying spectacle could completely uproot politics as we know it.

Momentum can have unintended consequences—not all momentum results in a positive outcome. Sometimes, momentum can create division or outrage. Transformation can happen, but it may not always be what was intended.

INFLUENCING MOMENTUM

The traditional media is a tool of influence, and its role is changing, too. News coverage in today's world is just as essential as a social media influencer like a celebrity or an academic expert. This is a big misconception in the world today. While social media and digital media is the way to spread information and gain velocity, traditional media is still the validator. In a world of lawlessness, somehow, traditional media has been elevated. There is a reason that Trump rails against the *New York Times* and the *Washington Post* as often as he does. He can't give them any oxygen, or they will gain credibility. He must continually expose their bias, or they could stop his momentum.

It used to be that we thought news coverage was objective and completely trustworthy. Now we've found out that it's not. In the same way, we used to believe that academics were objective analyzers. Now we find out they're paid. We used to think that social media was an honest broker of new products and ideas, but the influencers that use social media are paid, too. What we do know is that influence is powerful. People don't always stop to ask who is doing the influencing and what their motivations are.

As consumers, we have to be more mindful of who is selling what and why. Can we discern the truth in a world of Fake News and propaganda created by the best and the brightest? We have to use the metric of the thinking person. Does it make intuitive sense? Is it too good to be true? When I was on Hillary's campaign in 2008, she used to criticize Barack Obama, saying, "You can't hope for change. Change takes a lot of work." And the truth is, it does. Obama hoped for change, but very little happened. It is the same with this new reality.

Nothing is really new except for the access that people have to consumers. You can't *hope* that a product will work or a story will be accurate. If it doesn't make sense or is wishful thinking, it's probably just that—wishful thinking or Fake News.

Hillary was right about Obama. It's too bad that she was wrong about so much other stuff.

Media companies have known for thirty years that to keep momentum, they need to be in the game 24/7. Twenty-four-hour news stations have morphed into influence channels. Today, "liberal" and "conservative" media are doing battle for the hearts and minds of the people. They're not trying to inform as much as they are trying to shape our opinions.

Social media has given journalists a shelf life beyond their articles and segments, but it has also made them part of a rapid feedback loop. We know how many people read, share, and engage in the articles. They can no longer just write what they want. They have to write what will get traction and hence, the loss of objectivity. They are playing for the audience. Ratings become less important in a world of clicks and retweets. We can now measure how many people are watching or reading. Web content is a driver of interest. And that new reality changes the way journalism gets made. Along the way, old assumptions get crushed. There's little evidence anymore of purist reporting. People consume media expecting to be influenced.

In the past, when a single newspaper landed on your front doorstep, and there were only three news channels to choose from on TV, everyone saw and read the same information. There were strict rules about reporting—*who, what, when, where, why, how*. Maybe the absence of bias was an illusion, but at least there was an effort. Now we see supposedly unbiased journalists appearing on partisan talk shows to pitch their points of view and take sides. We see media empires being created to further political and social agendas. It can feel like the Wild West, but having the tools to measure influence means we also can hold journalists accountable.

The idea that everything is knowable influences momentum because it allows us to measure it. We can look beneath the surface and see who's saying what—and why they're saying it. With our team of data scientists and engineers, we use several sophisticated analytics tools and algorithms to understand the volume, content, emotion, and source of conversations. We can see how information and conversations spread across the internet and around the world. From my laptop, I can understand any topic, any conversation, in any language happening anywhere, and grasp its impact in a matter of seconds. Through sophisticated taxonomies, we can go as broad or specific as needed.

Before, we only had pseudo-sciences, such as Q scores, which measure fame and popularity. Q scores, a fifty-year-old technology, essentially only measure mass and give little clue about velocity. They're static measures. When you analyze momentum, you have a more accurate picture over time, reflecting the change.

KEY MOMENTUM LESSONS

▶ Mass without velocity is impotent. Both are needed for momentum.

▶ By the time something is a trend, it no longer has velocity. It just is. However, with change and innovation, it can start moving again.

▶ Everything is knowable, accelerating the way we find out what people think and feel.

▶ With the information at our fingertips, we can move forward faster and more confidently than ever before to get people, companies, and businesses to their best days ahead.

CHAPTER TWO

THE MOMENTUM MATRIX

H ow do you become a momentum-maker? Certain elements are reliable sparks to momentum. They might surprise you. Let's take a look.

THE 5 DRIVERS OF MOMENTUM

1 POLARIZATION: Competition and conflict

2 INNOVATION: Making something new and improved

3 "STICKY" ISSUE: Being memorable

4 DISRUPTION: Turning it upside down

5 SOCIAL IMPACT: Finding larger purpose

US VS. THEM

Are you polarizing?

Remember, momentum is value-neutral. It's not inherently good or bad, and while polarization is usually considered a negative thing, in this context, it means having two opposing sides, each with passionate advocates.

Face it, if everybody agrees on a topic, it's not that interesting. For example, as long as all Americans agreed that North Korean dictator Kim Jong Un was evil, no one paid much attention to what the crazy dictator was doing. But once Donald Trump began to hold summits with him, and even stepped into North Korea to shake his hand, suddenly there was a pro and con. Engagement in the Kim question spiked. People cared.

Trump is gifted in the art of polarization.

The press? *Enemy of the people.*

The FBI? *Traitors.*

Immigrants? *Criminals and rapists.*

The Democrats? *Losers.*

Polarization on both sides of an issue or competing product drives the intensity of interest, which is the hallmark of momentum. Momentum thrives in a competitive atmosphere, like two prizefighters in a ring.

Research shows that the more polarized the electorate, the more people vote. It's always been a question whether voter turnout is driven more by enthusiasm for your candidate or animosity toward the opposition. The answer is both, but animosity wins the day.

In product marketing, polarization is the fastest and most memorable means to make an impact. Product marketers also find ways to use polarization as a sales tool. It used to be that product popularity was measured solely by how many people loved your product. Today, with a concept called brand dispersion, marketers measure not just the lovers but also the haters. To achieve maximum dispersion, a brand must be loved and hated equally. A leading example is McDonald's, with approximately 33 percent loving it and 29 percent hating it. Low brand dispersion would be 33 percent loving McDonald's and 5 percent hating it. Smart managers today understand that having people really hate it can be useful, too. Being provocative—lifting and then challenging the haters—can reap results.

Some savvy marketers strive to create polarization where it doesn't exist naturally by picking an advertising fight. One notable example is a campaign by Miracle Whip, as bland and uncontroversial a product as you can imagine. Advertisers created a campaign featuring polarizing celebrities such as Pauly D. from *Jersey Shore* and political advisor James Carville.

Coke vs. Pepsi makes the most of personalizing the conflict. Are you a Coke person or a Pepsi person? People get pretty passionate about it.

The kiss of death is indifference. Indifferent consumers are easily swayed to try something new. I recently saw a cartoon by Tom Fishburne showing a group of businesspeople sitting in on a presentation. One of them said, "No, too polarizing. Let's go with the idea that makes everyone feel equally indifferent."

Guy Kawasaki, a marketing genius who counts among his credits the launch of the Macintosh computer, promotes polarization as the key to success.

"Don't be afraid to polarize people," he says. "Most companies want to create the holy grail of products that appeals to every demographic, social-economic background, and geographic location. To attempt to do so guarantees mediocrity. Instead, create great products that make segments of people very happy. And fear not if these products make other segments unhappy. The worst case is to incite no passionate reactions at all, and that happens when companies try to make everyone happy."

CONSTANTLY INVENTING

Are you innovative?

Momentum-makers know they have to be constantly inventing, creating FOMO (Fear of Missing Out) on the next big thing. Since momentum involves movement, businesses that rest on their laurels can't have momentum.

We live in a rapidly changing environment where the next big wave is always just around the corner. Apple's success has been its strategy of constant improvement. People might grumble, "What—another iPhone?" but then they buy it. They don't want to miss out on the latest version. It's the nature of technology to be edgy—and, in many ways, that makes this the momentum era. The intensity of product development, the proliferation of inventions, and the rise of tech companies are writing a new chapter in business strategies. Unlike most industries, the tech industry's very nature is innovation. It's what they *do*. If they don't have momentum, they're not doing their jobs.

The business graveyard is littered with companies that refused to change and innovate. Perhaps the most famous example is Kodak. For over one hundred years, Kodak was an iconic American brand, whose slogan "Kodak moment" was synonymous with photography. When the early experiments in digital photography emerged, Kodak turned its back on the technology, insisting that consumers wanted printed photos. It continued to invest heavily in its print products. It lost momentum and was swarmed by competitors who saw the digital opportunity. In 2012, Kodak was forced to declare bankruptcy.

Blockbuster was a stalwart of the retail landscape, whose innovation was the ability to deliver movies for home use. At its peak, it captured the market in video rentals. But an upstart called Netflix came along with a new idea—a cheap and efficient home delivery service that would make Blockbuster obsolete. Although Blockbuster briefly tried and failed to compete in the mail-in DVD universe, it didn't matter because that, too, was short-lived. Netflix itself might have gone the way of Blockbuster, once streaming services challenged its mail delivery program. But unlike Blockbuster, Netflix innovated, becoming the most popular and enduring streaming service available. It then further innovated by developing original programming that matched the movie and television studios in quality and content. However, for Netflix to continue to survive in what is becoming a crowded streaming field, it will have to keep innovating. Viewers are hungry for constant content. The big-ticket series, released monthly or even weekly, and the access to old programming, are no longer enough to feed the beast. What's next?

MAKE IT STICK

Are you sticky?

The concept of stickiness was introduced in 2007 by Chip and Dan Heath in their book *Made to Stick: Why Some Ideas Survive and Others Die*. Stickiness is another way of talking about getting people to engage with a simple, compelling idea. That's why products and candidates have slogans. They try to light up the public consciousness. Some slogans become so popular they outlast their origins and become part of the conversation:

"Where's the beef?"

"We try harder."

"Just do it."

"Morning in America."

"It's the economy, stupid."

Sticky issue momentum doesn't have to be sustainable. It only needs enough power to create momentum for a result. A crisis can help make an issue sticky. Thus, we designate certain calamities as "9/11" moments. On the other end of the spectrum is Trump's obsessive nicknaming of opponents to stick a label on them. It sometimes works, as "Low-energy Jeb" and "Little Marco Rubio" can attest.

In politics, a sticky issue drives votes, and a non-sticky issue slides off the public attention scan. For example, I doubt if anyone would disagree that the plight of military veterans is a critical issue. Yet no candidate has ever run for high office on a platform of helping veterans. It's not sticky.

Immigration is sticky, but it wasn't always. Trump made it sticky by creating a polarizing theme that engaged his base and infuriated his opponents.

Sticky issues are also crucial because voters and consumers often need a *rational* justification to make an *emotional* decision. We know that the decision about who to vote for president is primarily emotional—most attribute it to "shares my values." But people will say, "I like their immigration or jobs policy." So the stickiness is the issue or factoid that sticks with voters and justifies their emotional choice.

SHAKE IT UP

Are you disruptive?

Disruption has become a fashionable goal in business, politics, and social endeavors. The idea of outsiders shaking up the status quo is an old idea, but today's disrupters are carrying it to new levels.

Disruption is usually viewed as a bad thing when it is in the context of discontinuity. People like routines, and they like doing things the same way. It brings them comfort. But positive disruption has momentum. Positive disruption shoots down assumptions and challenges the status quo. It chooses not to play it safe. It can be scary. But change and transformation are the core elements of disruption, and they are also the keys to building momentum. Disruption isn't just making a small change or fixing a situation that is largely broken. Disruption makes us realize that things can be so much better.

In the business arena, Airbnb is an excellent example of massive industry disruption. Airbnb spawned the sharing economy at a time when people were seeking more affordable options for services.

Today Airbnb has more than three million listings in 65,000 cities. Uber was created in 2009 as a ride-sharing company, followed by Lyft in 2011. Both are disruptive to the taxi and limousine industry. All of these disrupters gained early momentum and rapidly grew to challenge the status quo. In the case of Uber and Lyft, competition between the two services has helped drive momentum, as each vies to offer unique features the other doesn't have.

Being disruptive isn't confined to new companies. Established companies, such as Amazon and Facebook, can gain momentum by disrupting their brands.

Disruption makes people uncomfortable, and that's the key to its momentum. It shakes loose inertia and asks, "Why not?" Successful disrupters can tap into the felt need that lies beneath the surface.

SHOW, DON'T TELL

Do you have an impact?

One of the most compelling drivers of momentum is the desire to have an impact—to change the world in big or small ways. That's true if you're a politician, a social influencer, or an entrepreneur. Your world-changing idea might be as enormous as sending citizens into space. It might be as ordinary as a product that makes people's lives a little easier, or makes the environment a little better, such as silicone straws to replace plastic straws. It might be as exciting as a policy that pays off everyone's student loans. The common component is *betterment*.

Naturally, making the world a better place means different things to different people. One person's progress might be another person's threat. Putting Susan B. Anthony's face on the $20 bill is a sign of women's advancement to one population and a slap in the face to Andrew Jackson supporters. Free college tuition might be exuberantly embraced by college students but seem an unnecessary expense to grumpier Baby Boomers. Making the world better can be subject to passionate polarization. However, making an impact can usually be viewed as a tangible thing. A decade ago, most people would have considered self-driving cars as a science fiction dream—and an apocalyptic one at that. Now the idea is becoming a reality. Its momentum is on the rise because it seems possible and even inevitable.

Making a difference has an altruistic air, but a better description is progress. Momentum is inherent in new inventions that capture the cultural imagination, solve problems, or take us to the next level. It is present in social movements that have a measurable impact—such as gay marriage. When people see reality, they believe it. Making impossible dreams come true creates momentum.

CHAPTER THREE

MEET THE MASTER
OF MOMENTUM

The 2016 presidential election would be the ultimate test of my theory that everything is knowable and that we don't have to poll to get the answers. We can just analyze the data.

Going into 2016, I had become disillusioned with polling. Over the past decade, polling had gone from predictive of elections to content that media outlets (cable networks, political blogs, and websites) use to fulfill American's insatiable appetite for political news.

How a candidate was doing in the polls was a justification of how well they were doing and then became the justification that they were the leader. It all became a vicious cycle of the polls predicting the polls.

So, as I began analyzing the 2016 Republican primary, I turned to social media volume and sentiment as a predictor. The social media analytics tools that were available were quite sophisticated—I could analyze nationally, by state, or even geo-fence into small regions within any state. Working with my partners at Talkwalker, I could write sophisticated taxonomies that would allow me to capture all keywords and associations. And unlike polls, which would take time to reach the respondents and collect the data, social media analytics could be done on an hourly, daily, or weekly basis. I had instant information.

It was by using this analysis that I found the power of the candidacy of Donald Trump. From the June day in 2015, when he rode down the gleaming escalator at Trump Tower to announce his run for the presidency, Trump captured public attention in a way few candidates have ever done. He harnessed the power of the internet and used it every day to build support. By using Twitter to start conversations, Trump created tremendous momentum—he was building mass and velocity constantly as people engaged, shared, and commented on his tweets.

Trump turned his social media feeds into news, allowing his crowd of supporters to share and organize. In this way, he transcended the media filter and went straight to the people.

In a *New York Times* article, "Pithy, Mean and Powerful: How Donald Trump Mastered Twitter for 2016," I called it the Trump Wall: "We've never seen this before in politics. This is not just a rally that happens once in a while. This is a continuous Trump rally that happens on Twitter at all hours. He fills the Twitter stadium every day."

But in capturing social media, Trump also corralled the attention of regular media. His opponents in the Republican primary—Jeb Bush, Marco Rubio, Chis Christie, Ted Cruz, and others—complained that they couldn't get media coverage to save their lives. The media was running an all-Trump-all-the-time show.

Trump broke all the rules and engaged the nation—on both sides. Whether you liked him or hated him, by the end of 2015 and going into 2016, all the conversation was about Donald Trump.

Trump was saying things that interested people. His words were provocative and even outlandish. People tuned in to hear what he would say next. His rallies were exciting, with an undercurrent of danger. In comparison, his opponents looked flat, like "typical" politicians.

In the general election, Barack Obama, finishing his second term, was not on the ballot. But Trump effectively ran against him, setting up a vivid contrast. Obama was so aloof, he said. So elitist. Trump was the one who represented the disenfranchised masses. *He alone could make America great again.*

Trump was such an outlier and an outrageous character that he was chronically underestimated by pundits, even as they gave him unprecedented coverage. Most people expected Hillary Clinton to win big—the media was telling them to expect that result. Hillary was experienced, stable, and had a mass of support. Everyone knew who she was. If Trump was often compared to a baby, Hillary was the grown-up in the room. However, the campaign turned into a referendum on Trump, rather than an elevation of Hillary. A campaign based on not being Trump was still about Trump.

Making matters worse for Hillary, the media endlessly beat the drum over questions about her email server when she was secretary of state. Analyses of press coverage later showed that the mainstream media bent over backward to provide scandal equivalency. That is, since it was reporting so many scandals associated with Trump, there was a sense it would only be fair to cover Hillary's so-called scandals as well. The problem for Hillary was that her misdeed stuck, and Trump's did not.

Negativity did not stick to Trump among his supporters because he was so adept at changing the subject—giving supporters something new to focus on. He kept the dialogue continually moving. He was adept at topic transformation rather than issue stagnation.

In any other reality, the *Access Hollywood* tape, a shocking, vulgar display of Trump's assaultive behavior toward women, would have doomed his candidacy.

Instead, it became a three-day story with no real consequences. Billy Bush, the broadcaster who was on the tape with Trump, lost his job. But Trump skated above the scandal. Why? Because he kept moving.

Three years after taking office, Trump's velocity shows no sign of waning. He remains the master of momentum, achieving the near-impossible task of keeping public attention at his beck and call. What is the secret to his success? He breaks the mold, defying traditional ideas of like/dislike. I wonder, too, if he is not just challenging them but redefining them, polling data, and public opinion. His momentum is something money can't buy and ordinary success measures can't capture. He thrives on polarization and regularly dispatches his critics with a unique mix of hubris and calculation. But his appeal is not just emotional, in spite of his supporters' fervor. Trump's practice of momentum-building is scientific. The metrics at play in analyzing Trump's momentum are rooted in science. It's not accidental. It's carefully calibrated.

TRUMP'S MOMENTUM METRICS

POLARIZATION: Few things define Trump as much as his ability to polarize. Few political figures can match him in the "love him or hate him" metric.

INNOVATION: Trump is an engine of change—whether forward or backward, that fact is clear. He has restructured agencies, collapsed traditional relationships on the world stage, and remade the courts.

STICKY ISSUE: "Make America Great Again" . . . "Build the Wall" . . . the Media as "enemy of the people." Trump's themes are consistent, and they stick to the public mind.

DISRUPTION: Upending seventy-five years of American foreign policy. FoP (Friend of Putin), FoK (Friend of Kim).

IMPACT: Remaking the Supreme Court and the lower courts will be a lasting legacy.

POLARIZATION GETS ATTENTION

Typically, political figures rise and fall based on the popularity of their positions and ideas. Trump is interesting because he flips the equation. His supporters aren't saying they like him because they agree with his ideas. They agree with his ideas because they like him. He believes that they represent their values. They don't agree with everything he says or does, but they can see the big picture. Their support for him is not based on a fact, it is based on momentum and his success. Trump is now a movement.

There are many benefits of momentum. It gives you permission to take chances and make mistakes. Momentum attracts people because they want to be part of the movement and the change.

Take the Wall. He made it the centerpiece of his campaign and his presidency. Chances are, his supporters would not be so feverish about the Wall if he didn't fight so hard for it. The Wall became symbolic of the larger perception among

Trump's supporters that illegal immigration was hurting our country. A nuance on illegal immigration was that it led to increased criminality, which threatened our safety and security. Indeed, none of Trump's supporters are criticizing him for (so far) failing to build a Wall. Why? Because the Wall was symbolic. Fighting for the Wall is fighting for issues that are important to them. In fact, at rallies, Trump tells supporters that the wall *is* being built, although that's demonstrably untrue. He's speaking to them in a language that they understand—in effect saying that they are building the Wall by focusing on the issue and not letting go. It is a symbolic victory, and he will keep fighting for it and claiming that he is building it because they know he is sharing their values.

This carte blanche support for Trump's policies is evident in other arenas. Unlike Barack Obama, who was a risk-averse consensus builder, Trump operates as a one-man band. He takes risks, whether it is stepping foot into North Korea (something no other president has dared) or starting a trade war, or calling American intelligence agencies unpatriotic.

Trump uses momentum to keep in the spotlight. That's why he'll tweet twenty times on a Sunday. He doesn't dare let anybody else take momentum away from him. He keeps it going. He needs the conversation to constantly be about Trump, no matter what the discussion.

Trump is aided in his momentum by a complicit media, which airs his every tweet and action. Ironically, Trump has been a boon to the very press he decries. In the age of Trump, the major newspapers and the cable networks, in particular, are doing better than ever.

THE NEW NORMAL

After Trump became elected, many pundits expected him to settle into the role and be a more conventional president. He did the opposite. Breaking norms became his method for maintaining and increasing velocity.

His Twitter feed, the subject of much scorn early on, even among his supporters who complain that he tweets too much, has become the daily viral method for commanding attention. He uses Twitter to air grievances, create news, and set policy. Every tweet, sometimes numbering dozens a day, provokes news stories. He has millions of followers, but you don't have to be a follower to see his tweets. They reach the entire population. Those who complain that tweeting is not presidential lost that battle. His supporters don't care, and the rest of the nation has come to accept Trump's provocative way of communicating.

Others asserted that once Trump's tax, tariff, and immigration policies began to take a toll on the manufacturing sector, in the farm community, and among immigrants who supported him (he earned 30 percent of the Hispanic vote in 2016), he'd lose momentum. While his favorability scores have never broken 50 percent, the Republican base—and elected Republican officials along with it—has stuck with him at almost the same levels as 2016.

The Mueller Report on potential conspiracy and obstruction of justice failed to make a dent. In fact, there's a lot of stagnation in the Democratic Party around this issue. Most people have not read the four-hundred-plus-page document, and the language is just nuanced enough not to make a firm case. The prospect of impeachment is of little interest to the general public. Trump just rolls on, doing as he pleases.

OBLITERATING THE OPPOSITION

The fate of the Mueller Report is a case in point. Step back in time to the release of the Starr Report, Special Prosecutor Kenneth Starr's 1998 investigation, which set the stage for President Clinton's impeachment hearing. Starr was a momentum-seeking missile aimed directly at the president. No one had a shred of doubt where he stood. Everyone saw it happening. But what did Clinton do? The White House strategy was to ignore the report and talk about issues, hoping to starve Starr's verdict of attention. It didn't work.

Now, consider the Mueller Report, Robert Mueller's investigation into the Russian influence on the 2016 election, whether the Trump campaign was involved, and whether Trump obstructed the investigation. The massive volume landed on Attorney General Barr's desk, and Trump was not the least bit interested in ignoring it. In fact, he gave it oxygen with his attacks. With Mueller essentially withdrawing from the public debate and insisting that people read the report, Trump had an opportunity. Trump's dogged assault and the AG's compliance became the story. The report itself felt like an afterthought. Countless public officials said they never even read it. Trump's version was the one people heard, and by the time Congress tried to investigate, the attention of the American people had already moved on. It was a master display of how to blunt an opponent's momentum.

THE BASE STRATEGY

We've established Trump's velocity. His challenge going into the 2020 election is to build enough mass to beat the Democrat. Although he still commands a high percentage of support from Republicans, the actual numbers of self-identified Republicans are shrinking. And Trump is also losing mass from Independents, the swing voters who were responsible for putting him over the top in 2016. He'll have to use his momentum to attract enough swing voters to get him to victory.

Trump's strategy throughout his presidency has been to continuously engage his core supporters, primarily comprised of older, white, blue-collar, rural voters, while ignoring or denigrating the majority of citizens. However, going into the election season, his campaign is casting a wider net, using the message of a strong economy to sell its message even to African American and Hispanic voters.

Democrats would be foolhardy to think they can compete with Trump on velocity. You can't out-velocity Trump. He's always going to be a more prominent newsmaker than any opponent. Where they can get him is on mass.

But it can't just be national mass. It has to be targeted in key states. In 2016, 136,669,237 people voted in the presidential election. Trump received 62,984,825 votes, and Clinton received 65,853,516 votes. Another 7,830,896 voted for other candidates. Trump won the election because he won in three important swing states. That could happen again, even if his mass is lower.

Because of Trump's momentum, I think it is likely that turnout will be higher, meaning that Trump's current state is not enough to win. He has to go to a future state. For these new supporters, it will have to be, "I don't like Trump, but I like what he has accomplished."

In 2006, I worked on Hillary's New York Senate reelection campaign. My role was to run a targeted campaign on Long Island. Why Long Island? It was the part of New York State where Hillary had performed the worst when she was elected in 2000. Many of the voters, particularly women, in Nassau and Suffolk Counties, didn't like Hillary. For whatever reason, Hillary rubbed them the wrong way. But they respected what she had accomplished (legislation for rearview cameras in cars to keep children safe, job creation upstate, and support for the military and veterans). Essentially, our campaign was, "You don't have to like Hillary to vote for her. She stands up and fights for New Yorkers."

Ironically, when Bill Clinton was going through impeachment, his stance was, "You don't have to agree with his personal values to acknowledge that his public values are good for the United States."

For Trump to win, he will have to get many of those voters who don't like everything about him, but who like what he has accomplished.

So far, Trump's base of support hasn't shifted one iota. It's not just that they believe in him. They identify with him. People talk about a cult of personality, and Trump has perfected that. He's saying, "Be like me. Wear my hat."

KEY MOMENTUM LESSONS

▶ Trump is the true master of modern momentum. He has used the principles to keep his momentum strong.

▶ Interestingly, he is the opposite of most brands that stagnate. His mass has stayed the same, while his velocity continues to keep going strong. Not always positive, but always in motion.

PART 2

THE SECRET OF MOMENTUM

CHAPTER FOUR

POLITICAL MOMENTUM
Winning Power and Elections

The 2020 election will be a momentum election. What does that mean? It means polls conducted before the election are meaningless. It means that the challenge for Trump will be to maintain his momentum and use his momentum on more traditional issues—a thriving economy, record job creation, and a strong military—to attract voters who may not like him personally but like what they think he has achieved. His biggest challenge as an incumbent is how to stay fresh. I already see a problem with his slogan change. "Make America Great Again" was a great slogan in 2016. It had momentum. It had drive. It promised to *do* something. The 2020 slogan, "Keeping America Great," is flat, denoting complacency, not change. It rests on its laurels. It doesn't move. Self-satisfaction does not create momentum. Voters are energized by candidates who shoot for the moon, not by candidates who preach the status quo. This is the perennial problem of incumbents, who are no longer the appealing outsiders that captured the imagination of voters the first time around.

For Democrats, *not* being Trump is unlikely to be enough to win. When I worked on the 2008 Hillary Clinton campaign, we spent a lot of time focused on "electability." The campaign spent a great deal of effort and resources trying to demonstrate to Democratic primary voters that Hillary was the most likely to be able to beat any of the Republican candidates. After eight years of George Bush, Democrats were ready to have one of their own in the White House.

Well, the early polling showed that HRC could beat McCain and Giuliani by a wider margin than Obama. But when it was all done, Obama won the nomination, and he handily beat McCain.

The truth of the matter was that, in January 2008, the issue in the Democratic primary was not electability, but Hillary's support of the Iraq war and Obama's courageous decision to stand up against it. It was Obama's inspirational campaign for Hope and Change. He was fired up and ready to go. Hillary's campaign focused on why Obama wasn't qualified to be president and couldn't win. Remember, Bill Clinton said about Obama that, "The whole thing is the biggest fairy tale I've ever seen."

By November 2008, the economy had collapsed, the housing crisis had put the financial markets in peril, and the US had to do several corporate bailouts for companies that were too big to fail. Obama had an opportunity to own the issue when McCain foundered.

Today's Democrats have to find relatable issues that motivate Americans. They have to find their velocity to move forward and then be ready to transform as the election gets closer.

It is incredible to me that the Democrats have lost their agility. They have become so singularly focused on railing against Trump that they have stagnated.

So, what defines a modern Democrat? Are they far-left progressives championing Medicare for all, decriminalizing marijuana, and increasing corporate regulation? Are they moderates who want to roll back Trump's 2017 tax cuts, and make higher education more affordable? What *defines* them? It's hard for people to get on board when they don't know what flag you're flying.

Obama was successful because he gave Democrats hope for the future—"Change we can believe in" and "Yes, we can." Obama created a real movement of optimism among voters.

Right now, the Democrats are championing pessimism. Interestingly, the candidates that do have momentum from the progressive side are using Trump tactics, just from the other side—Warren and Sanders are dividing America, creating polarizing momentum.

In a momentum election, pessimism won't work. So, what can the Democrats do? Bluntly put, they need to inspire America. They need to recast America as a great nation, a nation of doers and leaders who will command the century with our principles and innovations. They need to move into the space where confidence is sinking, where negativity and self-doubt have infected communities—and pull it out of the slump. They need to help Americans believe in themselves again.

THE DEMOCRATS—
A MOMENTUM-KILLING MACHINE

Sad to say, the Democrats have lacked momentum for most of the past seventy years. Their message is so diversified, they can't grab onto a clear and compelling message and make it stick. They have not had sustained momentum because they have not been able to transform. Occasionally, with a superior momentum candidate like Barack Obama, they're able to transcend the malaise. But it's unsustainable. And they fall back.

Going into 2020, they're still struggling. They have been searching for momentum in the fight against Trump—in the Mueller Report, in the hearings. Voters are not moved. Outrage doesn't sell.

Americans vote on momentum. It is an optimistic electorate that wants America's best days to be ahead. They vote on the future, not the past.

It's not that voters disagree with the Democrats' ideas. In fact, they agree overwhelmingly. It just doesn't matter because there's no velocity. Unlike the Republicans, who have a gift for unity and toeing the party line, the Democrats don't know how to speak with one voice. And they fight among themselves to the point that they are divisive.

The party could take a lesson from The Squad. There's more momentum behind The Squad than there is behind any of the presidential candidates. Trump has put a lot of effort into stopping The Squad's momentum. Nancy Pelosi tried but was ineffective.

THE SQUAD SURGES

The Democratic party gained congressional seats in the 2018 midterm elections. What the party didn't gain was momentum. However, individuals did. Alexandria Ocasio-Cortez came out of the election with a superstar profile. Ocasio-Cortex, who came to be known only by her initials, AOC, was a political newcomer who challenged Joe Crowley, a ten-term congressional representative from the Bronx, in a Quixote-style impossible quest.

AOC's momentum surged during the campaign because no one tried to stop her. Crowley underestimated her so much that he just let her go, assuming she was too far to the left with her socialistic ideas—Medicare for All, a Green New Deal, guaranteed employment. To the astonishment of political pros, she connected with the crowds and then gained sufficient mass to win the election. She was utterly authentic, young, and full of fire, and people responded. AOC capitalized on a particular brand of New York ferocity. People wanted to identify with a courageous candidate who never backed down. Then she gained national and global momentum as she started to engage on issues as a congresswoman.

In Congress, AOC broke the mold of the freshman edict to be seen and not heard. She kept her momentum going by being prominent on social media and frequently appearing in public to do battle with her detractors. As her profile grew, so did her enemies, including the president—although, notably, he hasn't given her a nickname. However, AOC's ongoing battle with Speaker Pelosi shows that she is not afraid to be disruptive.

Not unlike Trump, AOC steps outside the conventional bounds of congressional behavior. She shot a video of being a bartender (her previous job). She wrote about how hard it is to find affordable housing in DC. She videotaped herself dancing outside her congressional office, and posted it on social media, writing, "I hear the GOP thinks women dancing are scandalous. Wait till they find out Congresswomen dance too!"

She called out her colleagues for sexism and racism, always fearless. She has done something few congresspeople can do—she has resisted becoming part of the herd. She keeps putting stuff out to increase her relevancy, and she never gets stagnant. She didn't go into Congress and start acting like a typical congresswoman. Her momentum is so great that people refer to the "AOC wing" of the party.

Enter The Squad. AOC has joined with three other congressional freshwomen, dubbed The Squad, who are establishing a bold voice. Among the squad are two Muslim congresswomen from Minnesota, Ilhan Omar, and Rashida Tlaib, along with Massachusetts congresswoman Ayanna Pressley. Tlaib was one of the first to call for Trump's impeachment—and she used expletives. When you have this kind of momentum, you're going to be whacked. But these women know how to whack back with grit and humor.

The Squad caught Trump's attention. They perhaps betrayed his nervousness over their high profile when he launched a brutal attack on them, telling them to go back where they came from if they didn't love America—although three of the four were born in the US and all are citizens. This blatant attack on four minority women was criticized as racist, and Trump might have been deliberately signaling his base. It was a risky strategy. Trump's base is already behind him. The undecideds, suburban voters, and Independents might be less taken with the race-tinted taunts.

As The Squad shows, there's no middle ground when it comes to momentum. When you raise the bar on your public pronouncements, you open the floodgates for the critics. Masters of momentum know how to feed off that negativity to score points. For Trump to take on The Squad is to risk them building momentum that has its own colossal velocity.

THE SQUAD MOMENTUM METRICS

POLARIZATION: Not afraid to go on the attack, hammering the message against Republicans, Trump, and their policies—often with very bold and vivid language.

INNOVATION: A constant ideas factory, talking about issues of the future that young people can relate to.

STICKY ISSUE: Brazen oratory, radical personal style. They stand out.

DISRUPTIVE: Unafraid to put themselves on the line and challenge the way things have always been done.

IMPACT: The Squad has forced a reckoning by the Democratic leadership and the Trump administration. They're not going anywhere.

TRADITIONAL THINKERS GET CRUSHED

Democrats would do well to look at the lessons of history, especially:

- Traditional thinkers get crushed.
- Safe choices don't win (no velocity).
- Voters don't root for the underdog; they root for the candidate with momentum.

In the category of safe choices—compromise candidates—the walls of the Museum of Lost Elections are papered with the faces of safe options who fell: Michael Dukakis, Al Gore, John Kerry, Bob Dole, Mitt Romney, and so on. The 2016 Republican primary was packed with safe choices like Jeb Bush, Marco Rubio, and John Kasich. Trump dispatched them without effort.

Underdogs are only appealing when they have momentum. Just being an underdog isn't enough. Barack Obama began the 2008 campaign with clear underdog cred. He was a relatively new senator with a funny name who seemed destined to fill the fading outlier spot. His underdog status certainly didn't increase his momentum. What did increase his momentum against the Hillary Clinton campaign was his optimistic message and oratorical skill.

Obama had clear momentum skills. After two tough wars, a president that lied about Saddam Hussein and weapons of mass destruction (WMDs), and an economy that was faltering, Barack Obama inspired the electorate. He'd been building momentum since 2004, when he spoke at the Democratic Convention in Boston. "There's not a liberal America and a conservative America," Obama said in one of that speech's most quoted lines. "There's the United States of America."

That speech became a call for unity. It was the start of his 2008 campaign. Obama owned "Hope."

After an early 2020 primary debate, Democratic senator Cory Booker made the observation that when Democrats have an early front-runner, that person usually loses. It made a lot of sense and seemed true. Walter Mondale and Al Gore, vice presidents and heirs apparent, lost. John Kerry commanded the field in 2004 and lost. Hillary was the unstoppable front-runner in 2016—until she got defeated by Trump. Perhaps instead of a front-runner, Democrats need a candidate they can fall in love with.

WHERE'S THE VELOCITY?

In the 2018 midterms, Republicans lost mass, but they maintained high velocity because they're essentially the party of Trump, and he has momentum. The party will rise or fall in 2020 based on Trump's outcome. People are excited about Trump, for good or ill. No one would say that people are excited about the Democratic party.

Even the debates don't increase velocity because the goal of the debates is to build mass—increase name identity, awareness of positions, and so on. For velocity, you need more than twenty people on a stage, each saying, "Look at me." The competition needs to get tighter, one-on-one. Then you'll see velocity.

In organizing the debates, the DNC put all its emphasis on name recognition and donors, indicators of mass. This formula obviously favors candidates that are well known, above those who might have velocity given a public platform. For little-known candidates, debates are an opportunity to gain both mass and velocity, but if they're not on the stage, they're doomed. It's a Catch-22.

You can see why so many people think it's a rigged system. Are name recognition and early donor interest really the best way to establish a candidate's viability in what is a nearly two-year race? Are there better metrics to use in the early days?

Once the primaries get underway, those metrics are sidelined by the biggest metric of all—winning. Winning begets more winning. Mass grows, velocity peaks. That's when true momentum is possible because people respond to a winner. Sometimes all it takes is one primary victory or near-victory to give a candidate enough velocity to win. That's what happened for Bill Clinton in 1992. A little-known governor of Arkansas in a crowded Democratic field, Clinton wasn't close to being a front-runner. He'd already lost the Iowa caucus to Tom Harkin, who was, in fairness, a native of Iowa. Then, while he was still relatively unknown, Clinton got hit with a sex scandal when Gennifer Flowers publicized an affair with him. The Clintons went on *60 Minutes* to refute the accusations and pledge their loyalty, and the next thing you knew, Clinton was coming in second in New Hampshire after Paul Tsongas, who, as a senator from Massachusetts, was basically a local candidate. Clinton immediately dubbed himself "the Comeback Kid."

The momentum master of his day, Clinton went on to dominate the primaries and won the nomination. Gennifer Flowers seemed to have helped put him on the map. But once a candidate is associated with winning, as Clinton was, the momentum becomes unstoppable.

To gain momentum, you can start with mass, or you can start with velocity.

Heading into the 2020 election season, Democrats are trying to create counter-momentum to Trump. Is that enough to win? Is voting against something as powerful as voting for it? Starting with mass is death. To succeed in a primary, a candidate needs velocity. Mass will come.

With early mass, Joe Biden was on top of the Democratic pack, but he's not a velocity candidate. He plans to win by holding onto his mass, which is a risky strategy as a velocity candidate such as Elizabeth Warren has gained ground.

Democrats—especially Joe Biden—would do well to learn a lesson from Hillary Clinton's run. Heading into the fall of 2016, she was satisfied with her mass. She thought it was enough, and she never tried to gain velocity. Voters in key states saw that as a lack of interest in them. She was ignoring them—basically phoning it in.

Trump capitalized on that, asking, "Where's Hillary? She's taking the day off. She's taking the week off. Where is she?" He even added, "Maybe she's sick . . . she doesn't look well." That's a narrative that's crushing to an older candidate. (Not surprisingly, Trump has already begun making the same comments about Biden: "He looks different . . . he doesn't look like himself.") By the end of the campaign, there were questions about Clinton's interest in running and about her health. It was just enough doubt to turn the tide.

Sometimes, in polling, we can confuse mass and velocity, and velocity happens when you have a phenom that comes out of nowhere, who is starting to talk about issues that resonate. Who is the Democratic phenom that will rise above the pack?

Early on, many people thought that phenom was Beto O'Rourke. Beto was the momentum darling during the 2018 election, nearly taking down entrenched senator Ted Cruz in Texas. O'Rourke's achievement was so stunning that people immediately began talking about him as a presidential contender. But he spent months flailing around, off the grid, and as the primary season heated up, he seemed to have lost momentum to other candidates. As he grappled for a message, the narrative hardened that he wasn't ready for the national stage. By the time the debates started, he was considered an also-ran.

There's also a Bernie story. Bernie Sanders was a phenomenon in the 2016 Democratic primary. When he launched his campaign, people didn't know him that well, but thanks to his appeal to young voters, he captured attention on social media. Soon he had generated a full-fledged grassroots movement. A crusty old guy, he found himself the unlikely leader of a young following. He had high velocity, but he lacked the mass to beat Clinton in the primary. Still, his followers stayed in line, and when he announced a repeat campaign for 2020, early polls had him at the top of the pack.

We have lots of words for velocity in politics. We have insurgent candidates. We have rising stars. We have phenoms. We've had lots of words to describe velocity before without ever being able to quantify it. Now, we can. Insurgents are velocity candidates. These are momentum makers. They have ideas that resonate, that catch on. Then people have a way to take action. They can vote for them in the primary. It validates velocity.

Bernie's Achilles' heel in gaining fresh momentum is his failure to deliver anything new. As one commentator observed, you could play tapes of his 2016 speeches on a loop and capture his platform for 2020.

Bernie's other challenge is the competitive field among progressives. Candidates such as Kamala Harris and Elizabeth Warren speak Bernie's anti–Wall Street, anti-establishment message and have the advantage of being younger and more adept at public speaking. They're also women at a time when women are a force within the Democratic Party. If Bernie's message can be adopted by a more appealing candidate, he'll lose momentum. In 2016, Bernie had the advantage of being a lone voice railing against millionaires and billionaires. That's no longer true.

In fact, of all the Democratic candidates, Elizabeth Warren is actually closest to using Trump's 2016 playbook. She could be the Donald Trump of the Democrats for her ability to capitalize on polarization, spark innovation, promote sticky issues, and disrupt the normal course of Democratic politics.

THE FALLACY OF PURPLE

A decade ago, there was a lot of talk about "purple" states and communities—the idea of a middle ground where ideas from the left (blue) and the right (red) could be mixed into a less threatening middle ground (purple). For a time, "purple" gained momentum as a shiny new arena in politics where people could find common ground. While there are definitely swing states that alternatively go red or blue, they are not actually purple. Nor is the rise of self-defined Independents a purple indicator. Scratch the surface of an independent, and chances are you'll find someone who almost always votes Republican or Democrat. They dispute the label, not the candidates. For example, according to Pew, 70 percent of Republican-leaning independents support Donald Trump, want a border wall, and hate the Democrats. And far from being moderates, which is another fallacy about independents, they're rock-ribbed conservatives.

It's doubtful that independents will gain momentum because studies also show that independents are far less politically engaged.

IF YOU ARE NOT WINNING . . .

Remember Dick Morris? He was a big political mover during the 1990s and a Clinton King Maker. Dick always abided by the first principle: "If you don't win, you lose." Sounds obvious, but think about it. On election day, there is a winner, and everyone else is a loser. No matter how well you have done, how much money you raised, how many volunteers you have, or how you spin your defeat, it all comes down to winners and losers.

I was able to turn that into, "If you are not winning, you are losing," and that became my call to action as I went after new clients.

Three clear lessons could be drawn from politics that would be applicable:

- No attack could go unanswered.
- Everyone in an organization had to be aligned to a common goal.
- Always know what is next.

More importantly, winning started to become a dominant theme. There were winners and losers. Momentum was the sign of a winner, and those who were stagnant were losers.

KEY MOMENTUM LESSONS

▸ Winning and losing happen every day. If you don't know where you stand, you probably lost.

▸ To keep momentum, you have to have a plan for tomorrow and the day after that. So many people, companies, and brands rest on their success of today.

SELF-INFLICTED WOUNDS

Momentum can be fragile in politics. Although Trump has weathered storms that would bring down most candidates, he's the exception to the rule. If you look at history, most wounds are self-imposed.

I've always been captivated by Nixon's reelection of 1972 and the ensuing Watergate scandal that brought down President Nixon. I wanted to be sympathetic to Nixon and felt that those around him had poorly served him. Nixon had many successes during his presidency—he opened up China, he negotiated the SALT treaty with the Soviets, and he started the Environmental Protection Agency. I was not making excuses for Nixon, but it perplexed me that a man who had accomplished so much could be on the brink of impeachment.

How could a president who was so smart do something so stupid that would ultimately end his presidency? Back in 1952, when he was running as Dwight Eisenhower's vice president and got caught up in a scandal about campaign expenditures, Nixon had cleverly used the power of TV with his "Checkers" speech to build support among the public, and he was forgiven. Twenty years later, in 1972, Nixon had all the momentum—the power of the presidency, access to all media channels, and the experience of just having won a landslide reelection victory, with forty-nine of fifty states. He needed to move ahead, to keep building on his momentum. Instead, he did just the opposite, becoming paranoid and angry about his detractors. He obsessively focused on the people who hated him, to a crippling degree, and his advisors allowed his self-defeating behavior to grow until it ultimately brought him down. Nixon's tragedy was that he was on an upswing until he stopped his momentum dead in its tracks. He did it to himself.

Fast-forward twenty-five years, and people were asking how Bill Clinton could do something so stupid as to have an affair with Monica Lewinsky, an intern, that almost got him thrown out of office. However, unlike Nixon, Clinton survived. The difference was that Clinton navigated the impeachment waters by focusing on public vs. personal values. Clinton kept looking ahead; Nixon kept looking over his shoulder.

Howard Dean, who most people don't know anymore, was brought down by what came to be known as "the Dean Scream." In 2004, before the rise of social media, a single wild reaction collapsed Dean's candidacy.

Leading up to the Democratic Iowa caucus, the former Vermont governor was considered the leading candidate in the field. He was expected to run away with the caucus, but to his shock, he only polled third. That didn't have to end his candidacy. Many candidates have come back with losses in Iowa. But it's what Dean did next that crushed him.

Appearing before supporters, looking wild-eyed and overwrought, he shouted hoarsely, "Not only are we going to New Hampshire, we're going to South Carolina! And Oklahoma! And Arizona! And North Dakota! And New Mexico! We're going to California! And Texas! And New York! And we're going to South Dakota! And Oregon! And Washington and Michigan! And then we're going to Washington, DC, to take back the White House."

Then he screamed: "Yaaaaaaaay." People thought he looked like a madman, and they didn't want to nominate a madman.

The Dean example shows that if momentum is shallow, it can easily dissipate. If support is not committed, people might be looking for a reason not to support you. One false move, and you give them the reason.

Dean's fall led to Senator John Kerry's rise. Kerry never gained velocity during the entire campaign. He was a compromise candidate who generated little excitement. Despite President George W. Bush being saddled by war and beatable, Kerry couldn't bring it off. Without velocity, it's nearly impossible to take out a sitting president—a cautionary tale for the candidate that will take on Trump.

BEST DAYS AHEAD?

Barack Obama was a velocity candidate from the start. He was a dynamic, attractive speaker who talked about issues people cared about, and who captured the public imagination with his hope and change candidacy. And the specter of becoming the first African American president added velocity in crucial voter demographics. His velocity produced mass.

In today's elections, I think we give too much attention to candidates who have the most mass versus candidates that have the most velocity. Hillary Clinton had mass early in 2008, and she was competitive with Obama for much of the primary season. But Obama's velocity was too high for Clinton to compete with. The same thing happened to Clinton against Trump. Trump was a velocity candidate, and Hillary could not overcome it with her mass.

At our company, Decode_M (Decode Momentum), we try to focus on velocity questions: Is the country on the right track or wrong track? Are the best days ahead or behind us? Does the candidate care about people like me? Those questions indicate the potential for momentum far more than mass indicators, such as the number of people who show up at a rally.

CHAPTER FIVE

BUSINESS MOMENTUM

Catalyzing Brands and Trends

n 2004, I conducted a survey for a popular phone-email pager called BlackBerry. Two years before the introduction of the iPhone, BlackBerry had momentum in business, entertainment, and political circles. Based on my survey, *USA Today* designated BlackBerry a "Hot Pick" for 2005, writing, "In 2005, consumers predict the biggest winner will be BlackBerry, the popular e-mail pager that's become must-have equipment for movers in Hollywood and Washington and on Wall Street. Addicted users refer to it as 'CrackBerry.'"

"CrackBerry"—a word that captured momentum far beyond the norm. People not only loved their BlackBerrys; they *needed* them.

After the article appeared, I received a call from a representative at BlackBerry, asking if they could see the data. Realizing that this was a significant opportunity, I quickly said that we didn't share data, but I would be happy to speak to them, and maybe there was something more customized we could do for them.

I already had an idea—something that was simple and obvious to me. BlackBerry had a huge fan base in Hollywood, Washington, and on Wall Street. But where was Main Street? If BlackBerry was such a hot, desirable brand, it needed a consumer strategy.

In particular, BlackBerry was missing one of the most important and impactful demographic groups—busy women. And what woman is not a busy woman? They were missing women who work. They were missing women who manage families. And, of course, what about women who do both! Our strategy would expand BlackBerry from a strictly business device to a personal tool as well. It would target those users who needed to be in constant contact, who were constantly communicating with multiple groups of people (work, school activities, other parents, spouses, etc.).

In this way, we'd take BlackBerry to Main Street. Keep in mind that this was two years before the first iPhone would be introduced. BlackBerry would be able to dominate the market. The genius push email, fantastic keyboard, sleek design, and ubiquitous blinking red light would set off signals and create anticipation for its users. BlackBerry transformed our expectations for immediacy.

To this day, people ask whether BlackBerry made us freer and gave us more independence, or was the beginning of us never being able to get away—always tethered to a device. I love that tension.

And what about the nickname, "CrackBerry"? In today's world, it is doubtful that we would have allowed it to stick. But at the time, CrackBerry signaled just how addictive and necessary this technology was. While BlackBerry didn't promote the name, it also didn't take any action to stop it.

I ended up working with BlackBerry for more than five years. At that time, we saw tremendous growth, and it expanded around the world.

One of the most interesting conversations I had with the product development team was whether or not a BlackBerry should have a camera. Senior management at the time was skeptical. They couldn't see people using the camera, and thought it was an unnecessary add-on. However, our extensive research showed there was huge demand and interest in the camera—for both business and personal use. At the time, social media was just rising. Looking back, asking about whether we needed a camera seems like a ridiculous question!

Over the next five years, Apple launched the iPhone, which picked up market share and certainly set the standard when it came to consumers' expectations for applications. BlackBerry became obsessed with the iPhone. But the truth was that there was plenty of room for Apple and BlackBerry to coexist. The real competition was Android. And Black-Berry never wanted to acknowledge them.

Why did BlackBerry die? The short answer is that it failed to innovate. It didn't move; it hunkered down. It didn't understand the competition and thus didn't act to compete with fresh technology of its own.

BlackBerry never really embraced the consumer market, as we had urged it to do. Meanwhile, iPhone and Android were nimbly balancing professionals and consumers in their applications and marketing. BlackBerry was also overly protective of its design and keyboard, an innovation in its time that had outlived its appeal as people became more comfortable with touchscreens. It felt old-fashioned and looked dreary—like lugging around a mini-typewriter. Meanwhile, touchscreens allowed exciting visuals, video viewing, high-quality photography, and rapid data access. They appealed to consumers as well as businesses and organizations. They were in tune with a rapidly changing world of connectivity.

It was sad for me to see a company with such a commanding presence in the marketplace utterly fail to thrive. But the laws of momentum apply, even for those who think they have the market in the bag. *Move or die.*

KEY MOMENTUM LESSONS

▸ The market adapts very quickly to change, particularly when it solves a need. Expectations will reset faster than anyone can ever imagine. That's how BlackBerry dominated the market so soon.

▸ Unexpected competition can come out of nowhere and kill your momentum overnight. Android reached scale quicker than BlackBerry expected.

▸ If you don't give people what they want, they will go elsewhere. BlackBerry adapted too late to allow developers to write applications.

THE INTANGIBLE TANGIBLE BENEFITS OF MOMENTUM

In today's world, momentum does not appear on a company's balance sheet. But that doesn't mean that it isn't an asset.

Momentum does not have a financial valuation, but that doesn't mean it isn't valuable.

In fact, momentum is one of those invaluable assets that requires investment, maintenance, and management. And when done right, momentum delivers results throughout an organization.

Most of this book deals with the external benefits of momentum. That is my area of expertise—how momentum builds brands, attracts customers, and wins elections. But one of the great benefits of momentum is the internal impact and benefit that momentum can have.

I always take every opportunity to pick the brains of smart people I know. So, on a beautiful day after finishing a game of golf with my friend Gary Briggs, we sat down to talk about momentum.

Before I go on, I need to let you know about Gary. Gary is one of those low-key, silly-brilliant guys who carefully chooses the words he says, so when he speaks, everyone listens. His resume shows he worked at some of the most significant business operations of our time—Kellogg MBA, McKinsey, IBM, Pepsi, eBay, PayPal, Google, Facebook. His record of success speaks for itself.

I had known Gary for many years when he was the CMO at Facebook, and momentum was an important component of his brand management. I knew I could trust him to have some meaningful insights. As we talked that day about momentum, Gary scribbled his thoughts on a golf scorecard (which was all we had handy, and I love that. I once had a partner who used to write the most significant memos on napkins at Chinese restaurants).

But then Gary paused and looked me in the eye and said that the internal benefit of momentum could be as valuable as the external. Momentum, he stressed, is a huge benefit to businesses because, done right, momentum builds momentum. He told me there were three key benefits of momentum that he had discovered. When you have momentum:

- It is easier to recruit top talent. Everybody wants to be a part of the action. The company is seen as having its best days ahead.

- Innovation comes easier. It is a more creative environment that is willing to invest in the future and reward out-of-the-box thinking.
- You have permission to fail. The failure is seen as a bump in the road of success vs. a major event that questions the sustainability of the company. The ability to take risks and to recover from failure are keys to success.

Through our work at Decode_M, Lauren and I have also been able to identify other benefits to momentum from the consumer side. When you have momentum, consumers will . . .

1. Seek you out—they will go out of their way for you, line up for your drops, and eagerly anticipate hearing or reading your opinion.
2. Want to buy your products—consumers will purchase your products and proudly share them with others. They will become your best salesmen.
3. Be willing to pay more for you—consumers are willing to pay a premium for products with momentum.
4. Forgive you when you make a mistake or disappoint them—consumers are willing to give you another chance when you disappoint them. Everyone makes a mistake sometimes.
5. Want to collaborate with you—momentum attracts a crowd, and people always want to be part of it.

A company that lacks momentum will not succeed, Gary emphasized, but once you get it, you can't take it for granted. Momentum is never "in the bag." It requires constant attention, constant nurturing to keep it alive.

Sitting there with that scorecard, it occurred to me that we were following that last principle. Even after a fun day of golf, our minds turned to momentum and how to get more of it. That's something successful businesses do.

A FILTER-FREE UNIVERSE

Opportunity is everywhere, no longer curated in a closed system. The old filters have all but disappeared. Companies are no longer forced to spend large amounts of money on advertising just to get on the public radar. Before, a relatively small group of people controlled the momentum of most products and services. Today, the marketplace is wide open, and anyone can enter. Thanks to the internet, the business environment is more egalitarian than ever.

That's not to say that the competitive atmosphere is any less ferocious. In fact, sometimes it can be more so because with accessibility comes more competition, and consumers can afford to be pickier.

The metrics of *Mass x Velocity* apply every day. It begins with familiarity.

How familiar are you with a product? How likely are you to consider buying it? Would you miss it if it went away? Do you seek it out, and how likely are you to buy it in the future? That's mass.

Then we have velocity, which is really about what the audience believes and cares about, where the brand is going, and whether or not people want to be a part of it. When you have something with high velocity, you're sharing it, and you're promoting it—you can achieve viral surges.

So, mass is scale, and velocity is speed. They go together. One without the other doesn't produce momentum.

BUT . . . DON'T FORGET GRAVITY

When an industry soars, there will always be forces dragging it back to earth—remember Isaac Newton's Law of Gravity. Regulations, taxes, and community upheaval are among the consequences of great success. Just look at what happened when Amazon tried to build a headquarters in New York City. The community backlash was so intense that it forced Amazon to go elsewhere. In northern Virginia, where the idea of an Amazon headquarters was embraced, housing prices are already skyrocketing, causing early alarm that could turn into a backlash there as well.

Similarly, even as its products maintain momentum, the tech industry is struggling with blowback in communities. People complain that the tech stampede has ruined cities such as San Francisco, escalating housing prices, contributing to homelessness, and making the city dirtier and more crime-ridden. These consequences can have a real impact on momentum, especially if communities respond by overregulating, taxing, or by creating an unfriendly business environment.

Uber has faced repeated problems in the past couple of years—a highly publicized sexual harassment scandal and significant trust issues with its clientele. These problems haven't brought Uber down, but they have opened the door for Lyft to gain competitive momentum. Billing itself as "woke," Lyft is poised to beat Uber at the trust game.

The most significant force of gravity for the tech and other new industries is a regulatory environment designed to curtail phenomenal growth by bringing them back down to size and slowing their momentum. Deeply embedded in the American consciousness from the time of the railroad monopolies is a fear of companies or industries getting too big and powerful. So regulations are used to reduce mass and even stop their momentum. It isn't just regulators who are trying to do that. Sometimes controversy and a decline in public acceptance can ease the way for regulations. Consider Facebook. The deepening mistrust over privacy breaches and Fake News has led for calls to break up the company.

Having said all that, I believe it's also true that some things are tough to switch away from, regardless of controversy. It's easy to switch a drink brand if you don't like its sugar content; there are plenty of alternatives, and switching doesn't affect your life very much. But it's hard to switch your bank. And it's very hard to get off Facebook. You've got ten years of photos collected—how are you going to save them?—and access to all your friends whose phone numbers you might not even know. Quitting is a risk and a mess. In the end, companies that are hard to switch from have a built-in momentum advantage.

THE MOMENTUM OF A CRISIS AND HOW TO MANAGE IT

As we have discussed, most people who think about momentum see it positively. They think about the benefits of momentum and all the good things that come along with it. People are so desirous of momentum and will do anything to get it. But they're also cavalier with momentum and don't fully appreciate its power to build as well as destroy everything in its path.

That is why in my business life at Decode_M, when people tell me about marketing campaigns or brand initiatives, I take a contrarian view of what they're saying and let the data prove me wrong. When my clients tell me how well an ad is going to work, how brilliantly a sponsorship will perform, or how effectively a message will drive sales, I say, "Let me test it—from all sides, in all channels, among the target audiences and the unintended audience, and I'll get back to you." In this process, I turn over every stone and look at it from the opposite perspective. My job is to find the issues that others don't see and find the problems that others gloss over or try to explain away.

Why do I do that? Because if a program, initiative, or campaign tests well, I know that it is going to go well. But I also know that when it doesn't test well, and the momentum goes the other way, it is nearly impossible to stop. The reality of momentum is that it is much stronger and more intense for crises and controversies than it is for positive issues. In today's world, we must prepare for unintended consequences and be ready to harness that momentum wherever it takes us.

I am not sure that I am a genius for figuring that out. It is back to Newtonian physics. An object in motion stays in motion until a force of equal and opposite mass stops it. In most cases, stopping momentum is impossible; therefore, the best you can do is to apply forces to redirect it. And yet so many try with minimal prospects for success.

And this brings me to how to manage a momentum crisis. You can't stop it, but you can apply forces to redirect it to make it work for you. We tend to think of momentum as a positive, but momentum doesn't always travel in just one direction. There can be negative momentum, and to survive and manage "negative momentum," companies need to be nimble and understand how to use it toward its advantage rather than digging deeper.

Do you remember the Pepsi/Kendall Jenner ad from 2017? You know, the ad that featured seemingly happy, well-mannered young people at an unspecified "protest" rally. As friendly, smiling police officers watch the action, Kendall Jenner hands one of them a Pepsi, and the crowd cheers as the tagline appears: "Live bolder, live louder, live for now."

Pepsi planned the ad as a momentum builder, especially among Millennials. It certainly didn't work that way. In fact, some people have called the Pepsi/Kendall Jenner ad "the anatomy of an advertising disaster."

I call it a momentum crisis. Let's decode it. Quick note: all of my analysis is fact-based and data-driven. It is very important for me to separate my analytics and my ideology or personal opinion. The Pepsi/Kendall Jenner ad decode is an excellent example of that. The analysis reflects the analytics of the situation, not necessarily my opinion.

In developing the ad, the Pepsi team claimed to have tested it with twenty thousand consumers from statistically representative backgrounds. They showed it internally to younger staff members and received positive feedback. And why wouldn't they? It was beautiful cinematography, and Kendall Jenner was at the height of her fame. They thought it was a strong message on an important, topical issue.

But they didn't take into consideration that there were other sides on this issue, different perspectives, and different points of view. Yes, Pepsi raised an important issue and started the discussion that they sought. But they made a classic miscalculation of not looking at it from the other side: What if it is an average person and not Kendall Jenner at the protest? What if the protest was not happy and empowering but rather reflected pain and frustration? What if the cop didn't have a smile and became angry, scared, or violent? Yes, they sparked a "Live bolder, live louder, live for now" conversation, but not the one they expected or prepared for.

Some things to keep in mind about the Pepsi ad: the star of the ad, Kendall Jenner, is more memorable than the brand that sponsored it, Pepsi; and the discussion/criticism of the ad is more memorable than the content of the ad itself. Remember, in a momentum crisis, the story surrounding the issue will have more velocity than the issue. The momentum of this ad was the controversy and discussion that it provoked, not the ad itself.

That is the lesson we learned from the Pepsi/Kendall Jenner ad: when momentum starts to go in a different direction, you have to lean into it rather than avoid or try to stop it. When Pepsi saw the trajectory of the conversation changing, they needed to become part of the changing conversation. Instead, they stagnated and hoped it would go away. Here, Pepsi faltered because it clung to its notion that the ad was justified.

Here's what happened. All was ready to go, and Jenner proudly posted a preview of the ad on her Instagram account. The posting went live at 8 a.m. It trended positively for the next twelve hours, receiving millions of views.

So what went wrong?

Suddenly, a single tweet recontextualized the ad, changed the conversation, and shifted the momentum. The tweeter, who was associated with the Black Lives Matter movement, showed an image from a Black Lives Matter protest with a policeman next to a freeze-frame of Jenner handing a Pepsi to a decidedly more friendly cop.

The resulting momentum of the Pepsi/Kendall Jenner ad did not come from the ad itself. It came from the velocity of the controversy around the ad.

Many people believe the final scene of the ad, in particular, is a direct reference to one of the defining images of the Black Lives Matter movement: a photograph of Ieshia Evans, a twenty-eight-year-old nurse being detained in Baton Rouge, Louisiana.

The tweet started a powerful protest against the ad as being an insult to Black Lives Matter, which was engaged in police brutality protests that were far from the sunny portrait painted in the ad. Whatever the reasons, the conversation about the ad was so intense that Pepsi never even aired it.

The incident shocked the system of PepsiCo. Insiders were upset, arguing that the company had a very long history of supporting racial justice, and was heavily engaged in African American communities. Its then CEO, Indra Nooyi, was an Indian American woman. Yet, in one instant, that long-established credibility was challenged. Obviously, it's not fair to question a company's entire history and principles over one incident. But you'll remember our discussion from earlier: Momentum isn't fair or unfair; it's not moral or immoral. It just is. That's what Pepsi was facing.

Another key to momentum is that all the right elements were there: High Mass (Kendall + Pepsi) + High Velocity (Cultural Misappropriation + Controversy).

The question then became how to manage the "negative momentum," and Pepsi quickly learned that the same social media dynamics that changed the trajectory of the momentum of the Kendall Jenner ad also made it impossible to go away—the momentum was too strong. The ad was out, millions of people were talking about it, and it had stimulated a vibrant conversation that had momentum of its own. The controversy had more momentum than the original ad. Pepsi couldn't stop the momentum, and they shouldn't have tried.

Instead, Pepsi apologized quickly—delivering its most fervent apology to Jenner—and the ad was never shown on television. However, the conversation had already started, and hundreds of thousands of keyboard warriors were joining the debate. In the past, the media filter would have shut the story down after a few days. But social media kept it going, and Kendall Jenner's role assured it would be memorable.

Pepsi's apology actually made their issue much worse. Instead of engaging and living up to their promise of "live bolder, live louder, live for now," they were now patently inauthentic.

Was Pepsi's extensive research and focus group testing on the ad invalidated by the result? Not entirely. But it's clear that Pepsi missed the zeitgeist, which included the very issue that Black Lives Matter was leading protests about—police brutality in the African American community. The ad was viewed by many as a trivialization of the real problems Black Lives Matter was trying to address. As a result, the incident has become a case study for modern momentum. Most people haven't seen the ad, but they know the issue. It is culturally imprinted. It is also digitally imprinted. Although the ad never ran, you can Google it and watch it.

With all its research, Pepsi didn't recognize the reality of the tension between cops and the African American community. It ignored the imagined prospect of a Black Lives Matter protester handing a cop a Pepsi—something that was barely credible and might have led to a disastrous response. It even undermined its own tagline, "Live bolder, live louder, live for now."

An external force caused the shift in its momentum, and Pepsi needed a counter-force to change the trajectory of the energy. Why? Because it required influencers who could apply momentum forces to help improve the narrative.

But that didn't happen.

At that critical moment of crisis, Pepsi had a choice: engage and use its momentum forces to be part of the conversation or disengage and be run over by the momentum. It chose to take a conventional and ultimately ineffective path—apologize and back away. In so doing, it ceded the momentum to Black Lives Matter, and assured that the Pepsi/Jenner ad would always be viewed as a debacle for the company. For Black Lives Matter, it was an amazing platform to help millions of people understand their issue much better.

Imagine how the story might have changed if Pepsi had instead chosen to engage—had used the moment as an opportunity to lean into the discussion that had been raised by the ad. It could have said, "Yes, this is worth a conversation." In today's social media climate, a mere apology is not enough to stop momentum. In the eyes of many, it's just one more way corporate entities try to avoid accountability. Pepsi needed to do more to show that it cared about the real issues people were discussing. It should have become part of the BLM conversation and used it to engage to "live bolder, live louder, live for now." The best companies lean into their mistakes and learn from them. This takes courage, but it can be effective.

MOMENTUM LESSON

▶ In today's world, a story or discussion (positive or negative) doesn't go away when you don't talk about it. It has momentum of its own, and it can just keep going. The most important thing that you can do is to engage so that you are part of it rather than leaving it to others.

And maybe the biggest lesson of all is, as one executive told me, "Every company is five seconds away from this happening to them." Be aware, be thoughtful, be ready.

•   •   •

THE DISRUPTERS

Airbnb emerged from the ashes of the 2008 recession. In a time of considerable economic uncertainty, defeatism, and isolation, it became a community builder in the hospitality and housing arenas, disrupting the old ways and creating more egalitarian options for ordinary people. It was on the front lines of the sharing economy where people could take control of their destinies.

People have been home-sharing since biblical times. It's not a new concept. Moreover, vacation rentals have been a thing for a while. But total strangers staying with you in your home or strangers renting your house *is inherently an uncomfortable idea*. We are taught that strangers are bad, dangerous, and will harm you.

How did Airbnb flip this notion that was taught to us from the time we were able to process information? The strategies are numerous and quite simple, but they tapped into a felt need, the struggle of homeowners to make ends meet, and frustration with the sterile and expensive hotel industry.

Here are some of the key momentum transformations that launched Airbnb:

- Recruited hosts by playing into the post-recession/ gig economy narrative of earning additional income.
- Encouraged public reviews to legitimize hosts and overcome fear of "stranger danger" and other momentum killers.
- Interest and excitement created through social media and forums— making it seem like everybody's doing it. (Social media platforms

enabled a sense of belonging, allowed people to see the world in new ways, and brought people together to have conversations and discover new perspectives.)

- Created an accessible, user-friendly platform to connect hosts with guests and put everyone at ease.
- Focused on affordability and comfort: Why spend high prices for unappealing hotel rooms when you could have all the comforts of home and be part of a neighborhood?

In the beginning, Airbnb instinctively played off a polarizing idea. It didn't try to appeal to everyone but targeted discrete audiences who cared about authentic local travel experiences and were looking for something original. These edge travelers, in turn, legitimized Airbnb with larger audiences, creating FOMO (Fear of missing out).

Social media was a vital engine for Airbnb, highlighting an immersive total travel experience—the kind of support one might get from hotel concierges, but if it was more personalized and tailored to individual travelers. Suddenly, this form of travel was the cooler thing to do, disrupting the stale model of tourism.

You might say that trust was built into the scaffolding of the company from its early days. After all, they were asking people to take a leap of faith by exchanging the known security of a hotel chain for the unknown of a stranger's house. At the same time, Airbnb had to show its hosts that having strangers take over their homes wouldn't lead to a free-for-all—and they'd be protected if anything went wrong.

Airbnb had to scale to work. It was a process of empowering people at an individual level. Here are the ways they did that:

- Motivating hosts because, without hosts, there would be no guests.
- Marketing to potential guests, creating FOMO around a unique, localized travel experience.
- Making reviews (from both hosts and guests) integral to the process, thus establishing a sense of transparency that built confidence in the platform.
- Creating velocity from insiders who posted pictures and described positive experiences.

AIR BNB MOMENTUM METRICS

POLARIZATION: The hospitality industry vs. empowered travelers.

INNOVATION: Keeps transforming itself to meet new challenges.

STICKY ISSUE: Living in someone else's house—what a concept!

DISRUPTION: Democratizing the hospitality industry so ordinary individuals could participate. Disrupting the difference between tourists and locals—you can't tell who's a tourist.

IMPACT: Creating a new form of local immersion wherever you go.

However, like all disrupters, Airbnb ran into major barriers once it started gaining momentum. There were unintended consequences to its phenomenal success. As the economy improved, and the platform grew more successful, people realized that renting their apartments and houses was not just a way to make some extra cash. It was a real business opportunity. And local communities began to bite back and place restrictions on who could rent properties and under what conditions. Upscale communities railed against the transient nature of Airbnb rentals. Local media was quick to highlight stories of bad actors who trashed apartments or upset neighbors—or, conversely, hosts who misrepresented their properties. Suddenly, Airbnb became an easy target for politicians to blame for social ills in their cities. A new regulatory environment started to impact Airbnb's momentum, and there was a new fear that Airbnb would be regulated out of cities.

The regulatory environment created a negative vortex, where opponents of Airbnb—from hotel associations with deep pockets, to community boards, to politicians—were building a sense of distrust. Even residents who didn't object to Airbnb were crying "NIMBY," or not in my backyard. Although Airbnb had achieved significant momentum, now there was an organized resistance. It got to the point where anything Airbnb did in these cities, particularly in Europe, would strike a nerve and send opponents into a frenzy that would fuel the dumpster fires. The company had to figure out how to fit into cities.

Whenever a disrupter achieves momentum, the establishment barriers begin to rise, and to keep the momentum, the disrupter has to figure out a way around them nimbly. As a momentum maximizer, Airbnb began reinventing itself.

Sometimes restoring momentum requires doing something completely counterintuitive. That's what Airbnb did. Instead of limiting its outreach to those engaged in the model, it reached out to those who would never be a business target, to neutralize the opposition. First, it focused on explaining how it worked to reduce fear. It wasn't the sexiest approach, but it was a necessary form of marketing, and very smart. Maybe the audience would never love Airbnb, but perhaps they could stop fighting it. Airbnb began promoting the benefits to cities and local communities, flooding the zone with a positive message. More radically, Airbnb accepted a certain amount of regulation, which created more trust and built goodwill in communities that had been resistant.

In cities where this approach has been taken, public sentiment about Airbnb has improved, the volume of the protests has diminished, and the number of listings has remained stable.

YOU CAN'T BUY MOMENTUM: THE WEWORK LESSON

If Airbnb was a disrupter in living and travel, WeWork became a disrupter in work-life. WeWork, which launched in 2010, seemed like a deceptively simple concept for shared office space in a time when a lot of laid-off workers were trying to make a go of it alone. But it was so much more. Look at its mission statement: "Create a world where people work to make a life, not just a living." What does that mean? It turns out WeWork isn't only about providing office space to entrepreneurs, startups, freelancers, and small businesses. It's about forming work communities and social networks in the process. The desire for connection is a work-life value, and people whose offices were in their homes or who worked on their computers at Starbucks were missing out. WeWork provided value-added spaces for them to thrive.

With traditional businesses undergoing something of an undoing—laying off workers and emptying office buildings—workers were left looking for something more than just a place to work. WeWork grabbed the momentum in a new form of work-life—co-working. It's about so much more than shared space. The tagline, "Do What You Love" and "Love Your Mondays," is a better representation than the product itself. It's not just about less expensive space; it's about the opportunity of working in an empowering and supportive environment—something entrepreneurs and freelancers haven't been able to do before.

You may think that WeWork got lucky, given the perfect storm that the recession era yielded. What we know is that WeWork had a particular strategy that fits with momentum metrics. But then WeWork went too far. WeWork and its investors tried to buy momentum by valuing WeWork with a multiple that applied to a tech business, which they weren't. They claimed to have projected growth, which was unrealistic, and they used this evaluation of their financing as a marketing proof point for an initial public offering that didn't pass scrutiny.

Momentum is not for sale in that way. WeWork bought mass by becoming the top landlord in the five largest markets in the US. They did this by losing money, and there was a certain level of intrigue to their idea. But their valuation was based on their future potential, and their momentum was based on exaggerated claims rather than market innovation, which left them in a vulnerable position.

When WeWork filed for its IPO, its secrets came out, and its momentum abruptly changed from one of the most highly valued businesses to a case study in business ethics, self-dealing, and complications that come from misrepresentation.

As we saw in the Pepsi/Kendall Jenner case, the story of the downfall of WeWork became significantly more public and relevant than the actual business of WeWork. Many people know about the IPO failure and the outsize compensation given to its CEO, Adam Neumann, after his failure than knew about the innovation and disruption that WeWork had brought to the market.

The demise of WeWork and its overvalued IPO is actually not an exciting story. It's not the first time a company has been overvalued, and it won't be the last. It's not that different from the dot.com bubble that happened in the late nineties. Entrepreneurs create, funders promote, and investors should always be careful. Employees who took jobs, vendors who worked (myself included), landlords, and tenants who signed leases should have known what they were getting into. Startups are risky.

The interesting part of the story is how to *rework* WeWork and its future.

The first thing to know is that WeWork's momentum is strong. All tenants and landlords now know who WeWork is. Any brand awareness issues are over. Second, America loves a comeback story. Third, Americans are listening. WeWork has national interest.

So what do they have to do?

- Restore public trust.
- Have a business model that allows their innovation to continue.
- Hire a CEO with a public face.
- Stay true to their promise of an empowering and supportive environment.
- Don't overexplain it, just start to perform.

WeWork needs to apply forces to show the impact that they are having in the marketplace, the tens of thousands of people that are engaged, and how they reformed the corporate real estate world so that it could work for businesses and individuals of all types.

The bottom line is, WeWork has done good. And they should be allowed to be re-Worked.

WEWORK MOMENTUM METRICS

POLARIZATION: The association of co-working was directly in conflict with what more established companies care about—privacy, status, everyone in their siloes.

INNOVATION: Enhanced the trendiness and glamour of working on your own. Kept changing to design more advantages for WeWork communities. Redefined what community is about—not just about *meeting* people, but facilitating connections that help your business.

STICKY ISSUE: Co-working took off. It became a thing. Countries around the world wanted to have it, too.

DISRUPTION: Collapsed the economic barriers to procuring full-service office space.

IMPACT: Transformed forced entrepreneurship as a result of layoffs into empowered worker communities. Tapped into the way work is changing, with remote workers and more tools for collaboration.

A fundamental principle of momentum is that you have to keep reinventing to stay relevant. As things started to change, so did WeWork. For example, as some workers became successful, they were more interested in creating their office brands instead of being a part of the WeWork brand. So WeWork started a private office concept for "graduates," providing the same services without the branding. By continuing to build its company service model, expanding into other areas such as conference rooms and headquarters, WeWork understood that, for most companies, space is not the problem—the process to get space is. It's excruciating, especially when moving offices becomes a second job for decision-makers, getting in the way of their primary job, which is running the business.

Everyone talks about "the future of work"—and the future of work is here. As more companies embrace the new way of working, the benefits become apparent:

- Sense of belonging or "being in it together."
- Getting to a better work product/impact.
- Collaboration.
- Social engagement.
- Learning and growth.

The model was solid. But in 2019, WeWork stumbled, not because of its brand, but because of its snaky CEO.

SNAKY CEOS HALT MOMENTUM

Adam Neumann was the genius disrupter atop WeWork, a shining star in the galaxy of new-model companies. Everything seemed to be going his way in the summer of 2019—until he released WeWork's IPO prospectus, which shocked investors with its tale of financial losses and poor governance. It turned out that the company, which boasted a value of $65 billion, was only worth about one-sixth of that. In his "No Mercy/No Malice" blog, Scott Galloway wrote an August 16 post called "WeWTF." In it, Galloway says that any Wall Street analyst who believes WeWork is worth over $10 billion is "lying, stupid, or both." And from there, the dominoes fell. By the time the *Wall Street Journal* pounced on September 24 with a scathing takedown of Neumann, he was being ousted from the company. Neumann tried to stop the momentum of bad news, but he couldn't. Why?

The problems had been building for a long time and were deeply rooted.

Once momentum catches bad behavior, shady business dealings, or fraud, you have to respond quickly and get someone to vouch for you to correct it, or it will only slow down with a significant change.

Adam Neumann could not stop the momentum against him. According to *Fast Company*, "money, fame, and hubris, in the end, led to bad decisions, a toxic work culture, and now, a company on the brink."

Neumann had created an authoritarian reign atop the company, a reckless high life that broached no challenge to his dictates. His off-the-charts personal behavior was legendary—tooling around on his $60 million (company-paid) private jet, smoking marijuana in public, holding wild company parties, abusing employees whom he'd fire on a whim. His business concept might have been brilliant, but even a successful model could not withstand the daily assault of his leadership.

Fortunately for WeWork, the solidity of its brand might save it, and its business practices can be brought under control. Its radical disruption of the real estate industry is unquestioned. Could its promise be demolished by poor leadership and poor governance? In the aftermath of Neumann's fall, it now has an opportunity to regain momentum as the "comeback kid." Americans love a comeback and tend to be forgiving if a company shows it's serious about fixing its mistakes.

BEWARE THE SNAKY CEO

The rise of unicorn companies has created a cult of the disruptive founder, where the person at the top becomes the centerpiece of the brand. Like Neumann, these leaders are often defined by their big personalities, unconventional practices, and tendencies to skirt business practices. What feels exciting and new in the beginning can lead to trouble once the checks and balances of the business world set in. That's what happened to Travis Kalanick, the co-founder and CEO of Uber.

Kalanick was known to be a combative, damn-the-torpedoes type of leader who frequently offended partners and ignored advisors. He publicly railed against the drivers on whom his business depended, and was careless about the needs of his employees. Some of his leadership team accused him of lacking moral standards. And while momentum is not a morality game, morals matter when others are evaluating your business model. His takedown began when an Uber employee named Susan Fowler wrote a blog post about the sexual harassment that she claimed was epidemic in the company. The charge caught fire, exposing other flaws of Kalanick's relentless "bro culture." Eventually, Uber's board put the brakes on, and Kalanick was pushed out. There is no question that Uber lost momentum post-Kalanick, but its new leadership is working hard to stem the losses and put Uber on the road to profits.

Startup founders see themselves as rule-breakers, and they're not always so careful about which rules they break. In the early 2000s, Elizabeth Holmes was considered a hero of modern medicine. Her blood-testing startup, Theranos, was heralded as a revolutionary breakthrough in medical diagnostics, promising a wide array of laboratory results from just a few drops of blood. Holmes, who started Theranos at age nineteen as a Stanford dropout, had raised more than $700 million from investors, and her star just kept rising. By 2015, Theranos was valued at $9 billion. Holmes often referred to herself as the new Steve Jobs—right down to her favored black turtleneck.

In 2015, a *Wall Street Journal* reporter, who had been investigating Theranos's technology, began publishing scathing articles that fell just short of declaring Holmes a fraud. Federal agencies were also weighing in, alleging that Theranos test results were often flawed and statistically unreliable. The final blow came in March 2018 when the SEC charged Theranos with "massive fraud." By September, the company had dissolved, and Holmes was indicted. Her trial is scheduled for 2020. In this case, the snaky behavior of the founder crushed the company. There would be no comeback.

"WE CARE"

The corporate world is always trying to find sticky social issues that they can associate with to gain momentum. They know that linking their brand to a cause can boost support, especially from Millennials and GenX, who want to know not just the *value* of the brand, but the *values* of the brand.

According to a 2018 study on consumer purchasing habits, 64 percent of consumers worldwide favor companies that take a stand on social issues. "Share your values" is not just a political question anymore. For example:

REI: The outdoor company has redefined itself as a company with a conscience and consciousness, openly supporting environmental issues, saving protected lands and landmarks, and promoting gender equality. It preaches the need to adhere to core values and shows it's not afraid to make choices that seem counterintuitive—such as closing its stores on Black Friday and urging customers to go outside instead of going shopping.

Lyft: Lyft took a particularly strong stand after the Trump administration's 2017 ban on entry to people from certain Muslim countries, joining a taxi driver strike at airports and donating $1 million to the American Civil Liberties Union, which was working to fight the ban.

Dick's Sporting Goods: After a mass shooting at Parkland High School in Florida, Dick's executives learned that the shooter had used a gun purchased at one of its stores. It acted quickly, permanently banning assault-style weapons and raising the age requirement for purchasing firearms to twenty-five.

P&G: P&G rocked the ad world in 2014 with its "Like a Girl" campaign, a bold approach to the question of equality for girls. More recently, P&G's "We See Equal" campaign continues the fight against gender bias. An interesting side note: seeing the success of P&G's campaigns, its competitor Unilever decided to get into the act, with a ban on all gender stereotypes in its ads. And when the women's soccer champions launched an equal pay campaign, P&G was right there with a sponsorship, a full-page ad in the *New York Times*, and a check for $529,000.

Adidas: Leading the way in positive proposals to address climate change, Adidas vowed to use 100 percent recycled plastic by 2024, and has already sold more than one million shoes made of ocean plastic.

When companies and products are no longer "value-neutral," how does that affect momentum in commerce? How do companies choose the relative impact (for good or ill) of supporting certain causes or engaging in public controversies?

A NEW HIGH

Even a decade ago, the momentum for cannabis, which pole-vaulted it into a $32 billion business, would have been unthinkable. But it's a new world, as CBD (cannabidiol), an active ingredient in cannabis, is finding its way into a vast array of products and industries. Old-time marketers balked at the idea of promoting CBD because of its association with getting high, but this ingredient has nothing to do with THC, and nothing to do with getting high.

My firm came into this arena early on when a client, a leader in natural skincare and makeup products, wanted to take advantage of growing interest in cannabis for its skin hydration benefits. We used both consumer and influencer research to understand the opportunity and the areas of potential backlash for both product and communications.

It's not just beauty products. Cannabis's momentum shows no signs of ebbing because of its widespread applications. Hemp is being used in textiles, ropes, plastics, paper, and other products, with an emerging place in food and beverages. Some cannabis ingredients have medical and pharmaceutical uses, along with tobacco replacement and mood enhancement. Eleven states and the District of Columbia have legalized marijuana for medical and/or recreational use—and those states have reaped the rewards in revenues and taxes. The bandwagon effect seems unstoppable. It's a far cry from the time not so long ago when cannabis was so vilified that even hemp was considered scandalous! The momentum for cannabis has outpaced legalization efforts, but it's just a matter of time before most states are on board.

WALKING THE WALK

When it was learned that Stephen Ross, the billionaire chairman of the Related Cos., owner of the luxury fitness brands Equinox and SoulCycle, was hosting a high-ticket fundraiser in the Hamptons for Donald Trump's reelection campaign, there was an immediate uproar. This was a case of a company's brand colliding with its chairman's politics.

Of course, it's not unusual for wealthy individuals to become political donors or to host fundraisers. But Ross's fundraiser hit a nerve with the loyal following of the fitness centers, which were branded as a socially conscious community, supportive of women's rights and LGBTQ rights, and committed to social justice—themes that were at odds with many of Trump's positions. There was a massive outcry from members who felt personally betrayed, although Ross was characterized as a "passive investor," who didn't have a direct role in the company.

With a boycott in full force, supported by #GrabYour-Wallet, an umbrella organization for boycotting businesses that support Trump, SoulCycle made a determined effort to separate itself from the event. The company's president posted a pleading letter addressed "To our soul family," making it clear that the values of the company remained solid. It also announced that each of its 350 instructors would offer a free community ride to the cause of their choice.

Ultimately, there's little evidence that the boycott hurt Equinox and SoulCycle financially. But while most boycotts fail to do much damage to the bottom lines of companies, they can have a long-term negative impact on reputation, which ultimately affects the company. Equinox and SoulCycle are particularly susceptible to a reputation hit because of their socially progressive image. The internal dismay heightens the damage—its employees have been embarrassed by Ross's fundraiser. With so much competition in the fitness market, this can be a real concern.

The signs are clear that, increasingly, companies are held accountable for their lofty ideals, and the demand is not just external—it's coming from the inside.

Millennial and GenX workers are also driving momentum on workplace changes, seeking better conditions, more inclusivity, and accommodations to balance work and family. This cohort has made paid maternity-paternity-family leave a top priority. It's now a given that companies wanting to attract the best and brightest will need to have generous maternity-paternity leave policies and other work-family balancing perks—remote hours, on-site daycare, family leave (using time off for personal or family health needs in lieu of maternity), and even dogs. "Fur-ternity" is an increasingly popular family leave policy, which gives new pet owners time off to help their pet adjust.

My client Estee Lauder Companies has been a leader on these issues, even raising the bar to twenty weeks paid leave for US employees who choose to have, foster, or adopt a child, regardless of sex, gender, or sexual orientation.

More liberal maternity-paternity-family-leave policies have momentum fueled by Millennials, who are demanding work-life balance with a fervor previous generations did not. Millennials are not shy about making their demands. Companies wanting to attract the best and the brightest have to pay attention.

MOMENTUM MEETS THE ROAD

Since momentum is all about the future, which companies/ products promise to be breakout stars? At the top of my list is self-driving cars. When Lyft recently announced that it sees a world of 100 percent self-driving cars, no one scoffed and said it was impossible. From a momentum standpoint, the question is, how do we get there from here?

Consumers might have been initially skittish about self-driving cars, but the scenario has rapidly gone from "if" to "when." Behind the scenes, car manufacturers are investing heavily in retrofitting their manufacturing operations to accommodate autonomous vehicle technologies.

On the consumer confidence side, the primary issue is risk. How do companies get people to trust self-driving cars as safe? Manufacturers claim that safety is a number one priority because, without safety, the whole idea is dead. It's not just a matter of avoiding collisions. Smart cars have to be intricately calibrated to sense and understand their environments. They have to have better eyes, ears, and brains than human drivers—a surprisingly high bar despite the number of poor drivers on the road.

Few innovations have faced such a challenge from a risk perspective. Probably the best analogy is the airplane, whose rollout had to conquer public fears of falling out of the sky.

Waymo, Google's self-driving car project, has been one of the first out of the gate, and its cars are road-ready. Self-driving taxi service in Phoenix is already in operation, with "safety drivers"—a just-in-case feature set to ease riders' minds. Lyft plans to use Waymo's cars in Phoenix on a limited basis. In the next two to five years, self-driving vehicles will be a presence on the highway. Some analysts say that the mainstream use of self-driving cars is at least a decade away. Still, there is no question that companies who don't get on board will be left behind.

CHAPTER SIX

SOCIAL MOMENTUM
Changing Attitudes and Behaviors

G iving Tuesday (#GivingTuesday) is an example of dramatic momentum for making a difference, which began as a straightforward idea: using technology and social media to encourage people around the world to make online donations to causes and issues on the Tuesday following the US Thanksgiving. The idea was created by Asha Curran and Henry Timms with New York City's 92nd Street Y in partnership with the UN Foundation. Launched in 2012, Giving Tuesday has had a massive impact. In fact, it's become the biggest giving movement in the world. The key to its momentum was timing (capitalizing on the Thanksgiving spirit), virality (fourteen billion social media impressions in 2018 alone), and simplicity (ease of donating online). Its momentum has rapidly grown to the point where it is now an independent organization. Its millions of small donors are attracted to the idea of being part of making a significant impact.

It would be very easy for Giving Tuesday just to be one of those trends that gets built into society. Instead, it has continued to change, giving it constant momentum. It's re-invented every year, expanding to new countries and developing new themes. Giving Tuesday is all about the crowd. There are no boundaries.

It's a recipe for momentum. Compare it with strategies like the ice bucket challenge for ALS. It went viral, but it was a one-off. The ice bucket challenge was looking for velocity—an event that everyone would share. It was fine as far as it went, but it's not what we're talking about with momentum, which has mass and velocity. The ice bucket challenge had short-term velocity but no mass. It wasn't going anywhere. Giving Tuesday is mass and velocity, and that's the difference. It's got staying power, and it constantly transforms itself.

As an organization, it's progressive and future-oriented. It has distributed leadership, it's based on data, and it's solution-oriented. It also has the scale. In other words, it has mass and velocity.

Social impact programs often face unique challenges. People lose interest, or there are breakdowns in the exchange of money. What Giving Tuesday does better than anybody is authentically connect people. Facebook says they want to connect everybody, but they rip them off. Giving Tuesday is actually connecting people as a force for good.

A word about Giving Tuesday's leader, Asha Curran: she's one of the most impactful leaders of our time that most people have never heard of. Asha is a natural-born momentum maker—seeding ideas and growing networks. Asha is a behind-the-scenes person who is more comfortable behind the camera rather than in front of it. I met her when she was running the Seven Days of Genius at 92Y, which was a global festival celebrating the power of genius where people came together to discuss, debate, and incubate new genius ideas to improve lives everywhere. And the best part of Asha is that she is 100 percent self-made, starting when she led a babysitting collective for eleven families in her neighborhood on New York's Lower East Side.

GIVING TUESDAY MOMENTUM METRICS

POLARIZATION: Giving Tuesday challenges traditional charities, which only raise money for their particular causes, by opening up the landscape to thousands of philanthropic efforts. It's a face-off between old power and new power.

INNOVATION: Giving Tuesday thrives by not being a static concept, constantly bringing in new players, and developing new avenues for giving.

STICKY ISSUE: The Tuesday after Thanksgiving is a date everyone can remember, and it's also when people are in a giving mood.

DISRUPTIVE: Philanthropy typically operates within a closed system, with many thousands of discrete entities raising funds. Giving Tuesday explodes the model.

IMPACT: The dispersion of billions of dollars around the world to do good is the definition of social impact.

#METOO'S MOJO

The slow drumbeat heralding the #MeToo movement had been building for years with a spattering of lawsuits, allegations of sexual improprieties among powerful people, and the ouster of Roger Ailes from Fox News after Gretchen Carlson filed a sexual harassment lawsuit. But the issue of sexual harassment still lacked momentum—until October 2017, when detailed allegations against movie mogul Harvey Weinstein hit the news and social media with a hashtag, #MeToo. The hashtag captured the core message of the issue: sexual harassment wasn't an isolated issue; it was a common one. In the first day of its appearance, #MeToo was retweeted 200,000 times.

In the weeks following Harvey Weinstein's fall, the floodgates opened. One after another of America's most influential men—Matt Lauer, Charlie Rose, Louis C.K., Morgan Freeman, Les Moonves, Al Franken, Tony Robbins, Bryan Singer, James Franco, Steve Wynn, and Tom Brokaw, among others—stumbled after charges of sexual harassment were made against them.

Initially, #MeToo might have been a cathartic clearing of the air and a rallying cry for women's empowerment. But was it a movement with longevity? Could it change the world? These are essential questions because what seem to be burning issues can quickly flame out and die after the initial surge of interest. Within a year of #MeToo's entry into the vernacular, the issue had all but disappeared. Why?

A movement cannot self-sustain based on a negative goal—in this case, to expose and bring down sexual harassers. A public curiosity nourished the initial interest about the celebrities involved, but over time even that's not enough. Even a nobler goal—to empower women—is too vague and undefined to drive momentum.

A similar thing happened after a former student at Marjory Stoneman Douglas High School in Parkland, Florida, opened fire, killing seventeen students on February 14, 2018. By the following day, bright, media-savvy students were on the air taking on the gun manufacturers and the politicians they funded. Their campaign, tagged #NeverAgain, continued to gain momentum, fueled by massive rallies, a social media campaign, and a voter registration drive aimed at defeating NRA-backed candidates in the midterm election.

The success of the campaign was realized at the ballot box, where at least a dozen NRA-endorsed candidates lost their congressional races. But after the election, the momentum stalled. In reality, gun control is an example of an issue that has struggled to be sticky, despite the frequency and horror of mass shootings. That being said, the attacks on the NRA seemed to hit the mark. Throughout 2018 and into 2019, the NRA has been losing momentum—sponsors, money, support, and reputation. According to Robert Spitzer, a political scientist and expert on gun laws, the NRA might have lost its ability to be an influencer in the 2020 election. "The NRA may recover from this," he said. "They've recovered before from adversity. But their current problems put them in a bad position in respect to 2020." Maybe the Parkland kids got it right in one respect, but bringing down the NRA hasn't budged legislation on gun control.

Sometimes significant issues like gun control lose momentum because they're complex; they have a vague endgame; they're up against the counter-momentum of people on the other side who have an effective, if inaccurate, message that the government wants to take their guns away; and they're subject to congressional action, which sends politicians into a duck-and-cover mode to appease constituents.

In my mind, there's one overarching reason that #Never-Again was going to lose momentum: there's no plausible endpoint. Social issue momentum relies on a satisfying win in the same way political momentum relies on a candidate being victorious. At first, #MeToo wins were recognized in criminal justice actions against Weinstein. But the movement was much bigger than Weinstein. Seeing a sexual harasser get fired might have created momentum for a day or two, but it didn't last. People began to wonder if the excessive focus on inappropriate workplace behaviors—no matter how small—was unfairly targeting men and contributing to more fear and hostility at work.

LGBTQ rights are vague in the same way as #MeToo. However, same-sex marriage was highly specific and attainable. The momentum for the right to marry was forceful in 2014 and 2015, leading to a Supreme Court decision requiring the states to recognize same-sex marriage.

KEEP MOVING

So, what's the difference between a movement and momentum? Is a movement sustained momentum? The key to maintaining movement momentum is easy to identify but hard to execute: you have to keep investing, keep working, keep building support—long after the first flush of excitement. At the same time, you have to be preparing for the long haul. You have to be preparing to build and organize mass.

Momentum needs a constant feed to keep the velocity. Often, the way to get velocity is to move past the original idea and create something new. The women's movement has faltered because it never expanded beyond its original concept of equal rights. Equal rights are a worthy goal; the problem is, its repetition over the decades has made it seem stale. You can't build momentum on stale themes. You have to find new positive energy. And that can't come from merely articulating what you're against. You have to say what you're for—and it has to be specific. People have to be able to im-

agine a result. A perfect example of that is the women's suf-
frage movement. There was a clear goal: the right to vote.
There was no doubt in anyone's mind what the movement
stood for. There was an endpoint when women won the right
to vote, which happened in 1920. The momentum never
waned until the goal was reached.

Another momentum-challenged issue is abortion. Even
though the matter seemed resolved by the Supreme Court,
the anti-abortion—or pro-life—organizers have been working for fifty years to banish abortion from the earth. The
anti-abortion movement has executed a near-perfect long
game. They achieve a spark of momentum when the climate
is favorable, then work steadily on the ground to build a
legislative path in friendly states.

One reason climate change is a complicated issue from a
momentum standpoint is that it's hard to picture the end
goal. It's a sticky issue with a lot of support but little clarity.
Fear of vague catastrophes at unknown future dates is not
enough to galvanize the level of movement activity needed
for change. And the surprising continued strength of the
anti-science movement has made it difficult to get the message across. Short of catastrophe, the best way for these
broader issues to gain momentum is to narrow the focus to
specific topics. The key is to give people a goal that can be
realized.

I've heard people say that the issue of climate change
won't gain momentum until there is an enormous catastrophe, too great to ignore—volcanos obliterating communities, coastline cities disappearing, drought massively
destroying farms. Disasters can be good at coalescing people
behind a cause or a mission—as 9/11 did. It's hard to predict
what would be a big enough disaster to force a consensus
around climate change.

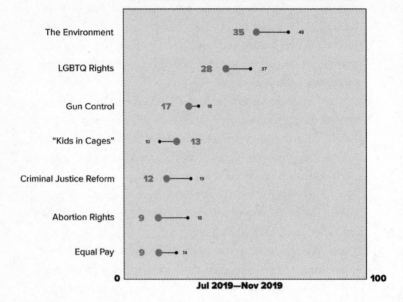

Which Social Movements Have the Most Momentum?

The Environment — 35 ● 48

LGBTQ Rights — 28 ● 37

Gun Control — 17 ● 18

"Kids in Cages" — 10 ● 13

Criminal Justice Reform — 12 ● 19

Abortion Rights — 9 ● 18

Equal Pay — 9 ● 14

0   Jul 2019–Nov 2019   100

CHAPTER SEVEN

SPORTS MOMENTUM
The Science of Winning

The player steps up to the plate, and the crowd cheers with wild abandon. It's the sixth inning, the game is tied, and the man up to bat has hit a single and a home run in previous at bats. Now the crowd senses that he's in the zone—he has *momentum*. Their loud cries, the stomping of thousands of feet, the shouts of "Let's go . . . let's go," are meant to lift him into a decisive moment. His teammates are on their feet in the dugout, waiting for the crack of bat against ball.

The dynamic is often called psychological momentum, and it is a cornerstone of competitive sports. It is the belief that previous success creates an unstoppable drive to further successes. But is this momentum an illusion? Is a winning streak self-perpetuating, or is it the product of fantasy? To be sure, it is a wish fulfilled often enough to seem real.

Momentum, in the sense of a psychological lift, is so inherent in our view of sports that it's hard to talk about it any other way. We conveniently discount the myriad examples when the lift doesn't come—when the baseball team's hot hitter strikes out during his third at bat, when the football team that is dominating the game loses in the last few seconds after the opposing team achieves unexpected momentum of its own.

I've experienced the same dynamic running marathons. At some point in a twenty-six-mile run, my body seems to achieve a momentum that drives it beyond all exhaustion to the finish line—a second wind. The sheer will to move forward transmits to the feet, and I keep going. In the same way, a boxer in the ring might push through blurred eyes and blood to explode in a knockout punch. The explanation might be adrenaline, a factor in the fight-or-flight instinct. It's also an example of force applied to velocity.

This trust we have in sports momentum is almost romantic. However, unlike the science of momentum, these psychological surges are unpredictable, and defeat is just as likely as a success. That's not to say that there are no elements of science in sports momentum. But we have to look beyond the player to the game.

CRUNCHING THE NUMBERS

In baseball, superstition reigns. Avid fans have long believed that specific rules apply on the road to victory. For example, talking about a no-hitter while it's in progress can jinx the pitcher. Or wearing your lucky shirt to the ballpark will help your team's chances. The players themselves are notorious for their quirks and rituals meant to improve their chances—everything from special underwear to ritualistic preparations for a game. These mystical interventions have been a constant in baseball culture. There is also a deeply held belief that the fans in the stands can move a team's momentum, by cheering, clapping in sync, or doing the wave.

In sports, momentum has long been considered a matter of emotion and mental preparedness. As the hall of fame catcher Yogi Berra put it, "Baseball is 90 percent mental. The other half is physical."

But increasingly, momentum in baseball has become a matter of analytics. Here, everything is knowable, including how a hitter will hit, a pitcher will pitch, and a fielder will field in any given circumstance. Where the RBIs and ERAs were once the primary measures of a player's success and potential, now the focus has broadened. Players can get data down to the micro-level—when to use certain pitches, when is the optimal time to steal a base, which players face off best against certain competitors, and so on. A whole series of measures go through the analytical screen.

As marketing analyst Ryan Woodhouse observed, "Once upon a time, all of a player's important stats could fit on the back of a baseball card. Now it seems like we're not satisfied until we know how many extra-base hits [New York Yankees outfielder] Aaron Judge gets during Tuesday's away games with his left shoe untied."

Baseball analytics is not a perfect science. Even the teams who swear by it haven't quite cracked the code of individual players' quirks and abilities. Still, using analytics to examine each moment in the life of a game, teams can provide players with real-time evidence of what works and doesn't work. Increasingly, professional and college teams across all sports are employing analytics professionals.

Analytics is not just about zeroing in on individual players. It covers the terrain—game preparation, roster strategy, scouting strategies and draft analysis, and even marketing and community relations. It's not just the coach with a clipboard anymore.

Analytics can help explain momentum. For example, why are some players so good in the regular season, and then they stink in the playoffs? It's because, in the regular season, the rotation is more set, and chances are they're not facing the best pitchers all the time. Often, they're facing the worst pitchers, the most tired pitchers, and it's a significantly easier game. Then, in the playoffs and the World Series, they face the best pitchers. It can be as simple as that, although some hitters do better against better pitchers. With analytics, it's all known. It becomes a numbers game that has more to do with the circumstances than the individual player.

Ever since 2003, when Michael Lewis wrote *Moneyball* (which was made into a movie starring Brad Pitt), people have been talking about sports analytics. Team momentum in the future will most certainly be based to some degree on analytics. Will analytics rob the game of its magic? Already, some observers, including former baseball greats, are complaining that analytics have made the game longer and more boring— one reason for a decline in attendance. Too many relief pitchers, too many home runs, too much time between pitches.

But the analytics model is not sustainable. The new momentum is with player and team development, more than analytics. It's not just about figuring out the numbers and the odds. It's about moving forward and creating the future. In his book *The MVP Machine: How Baseball's New Nonconformists Are Using Data to Build Better Players*, Ben Lindbergh describes a new philosophy of human potential. It's no longer enough to have innate physical talent. The momentum is in maximizing talent. The focus becomes on how to build skills on a micro level.

TEAM LOYALTY: ULTIMATE BRANDING

Completely apart from the question of victory and defeat is the question of the fan base. Sports teams are like brands, and fans are consumers of those brands. In some respects, they exhibit typical behaviors of brand loyalty, such as a strong emotional attachment and repeat purchases. However, unlike other products, their loyalty to them often transcends performance. They are extraordinarily forgiving of poor performance—the "lovable loser" syndrome. So, to inspire loyalty, a team doesn't necessarily have to win in a given year. Fans are willing to wait it out, to play the long game, to look optimistically to the future. This is especially true of fanatical fans whose social identity is tied to their affiliation with their team. Their participation is a critical part of their identity and their community. They'll complain about their team and even boo it, but they'll keep coming back, chasing the glorious moment when victory will be achieved.

In an unusual twist, fans of losing teams even exhibit some pride in the struggle. They are contemptuous of the cushy fan base of perennial winners like the New York Yankees or the New England Patriots. Unlike the elite winners, they have a tough road. It's a daily battle. Being a fan is hard work, and they are proud of their participation. Anyone can love a winner; it takes special grit to love a loser. They revel in the rushing emotion of each loss—especially the big losses—sharing the funereal despair with their "family" of fans. But heartbreak lasts only as long as it takes to pick themselves up and proclaim that next year will be different.

Dr. Edward Hirt, a professor with the Department of Psychological and Brain Sciences at Indiana University, has researched fan behavior. "We truly embrace having other people commiserate with us," he observed. "It's a real bonding thing to feel connected with people who care as much as you do. You get that win, lose, or draw with sports. What a great opportunity to feel connected to something that transcends ourselves." And there's always hope. The thing about sports is that anything can happen on a given day, analytics be damned.

Fan loyalty is intensified by the understanding that their teams *need* them to win. Players reinforce this by crediting their wins to the enthusiastic support of fans in the stands. And there might be some science behind the momentum of victory. At least one study showed that visiting soccer teams, with few fans in the stands, were 20 percent less likely to win.

Fan loyalty has enduring momentum because it is always focused on the future—the possibility that next year will be different.

Fans love underdog teams because the thrill of victory, if it comes, is so great. After the most recent New England Patriots (predictable) win in the Super Bowl, the *Boston Globe* reported that there was only muted excitement in the city. Maybe they're tired of all the winning.

For decades, the Washington Capitals were the lovable losers of the National Hockey League, under the leadership of their dedicated leader, Ted Leonsis. When Leonsis bought the team in 1999, he vowed to win the Stanley Cup. But year after year, the team went down to defeat. For almost twenty years, Leonsis invested in his team, developed his players, and sought victory. And each year, the team went down to defeat.

Loyal fans of the Capitals never gave up. In fact, the Capitals sold out more than four hundred games leading up to 2018—the year they were finally victorious. Leonsis portrayed the long, arid drive to success as being an epic battle that made success so much more rewarding. "It is much, much sweeter to go through all the pain and suffering to get to the top of the mountain," he said. "That's the way great businesses get built. It's never easy."

MASTERING MOMENTUM LEADERSHIP

How do you learn leadership? Where is leadership taught? The military does an amazing job instilling leadership—but that is a special type of leader. Jack Welch seems to be making a second career in teaching leadership through his Jack Welch Management Institute.

But who is teaching momentum leadership? The dedication to continuous transformation to get to the next level? The willingness to take chances with the successes and inevitable failures that come with it? The commitment to the success of the organization no matter what the personal cost to the leader?

As I moved through my career, it was clear to me that leadership is a critical element of making momentum matter.

There are five key characteristics of momentum leadership:

- Vision
- Authenticity
- Commitment to doing what is right, not just what is popular
- Risk-taking, willingness to fail
- Empowering your team and having their back

One of the most impactful momentum leaders that I've met over my career is Gary Bettman, commissioner of the National Hockey League. I worked at the NHL for the 2008 to 2009 season. As head of communications, I was able to experience Bettman's leadership firsthand.

Bettman may not be the most popular person in hockey. In fact, he is commonly booed by fans when he awards the Stanley Cup to the winning team. But in all situations, Bettman's personal values and commitment to what he thinks is right inspire all of those around him. Bettman has an authenticity that cannot be matched.

Bettman has been commissioner of the National Hockey League for the past twenty-six years. In that time, the league's revenue has gone from $400 million to $5 billion. The number of teams has increased from twenty-four to thirty-one. The NHL was the first league to have a team in Las Vegas, breaking the barrier for the other leagues.

Hockey is a sport of tradition with a passionate fan base. Bettman has kept the league moving in the right direction with rule changes that have led to an increase in goal scoring and made the game faster on the ice. His innovations of a series of outdoor games, hockey games in China, and teams in non-traditional hockey cities has grown the game and brought in new fans.

Very few of the changes and innovations were embraced at first, but most have had a significant positive effect on the league and the sport.

But it's Bettman's constant drive to challenge his team at league headquarters to question the status quo—why they have to do things the way they've always been done—that drives the league's momentum. He encourages them to make bold decisions and then has their back. He is an example of momentum leadership: not always popular but constantly moving in the right direction and growing.

CHAPTER EIGHT

PERSONAL MOMENTUM

Secrets of Happiness

I met Dr. Mehmet Oz a few years ago when he was encountering blowback on his credibility. Because Oz was a ubiquitous presence, a national counselor on the health of the nation, he was prone to be exploited on the internet with the use of his image and endorsements. He needed a way to restore his image as "America's doctor."

I was utterly taken with this incredible man who had an unerring understanding of people, their motivations, and their vast stores of compassion. He cared about people, he cared about a multitude of issues, and he especially cared about health care. He was engaged and accessible. I could see that one of the reasons he was being attacked was that he was making doctors look bad. In an era where health care had become a transactional business, and doctors didn't have enough time to see patients, Dr. Oz was the person on TV who became the viewers' de facto doctor. My best advice to him was to focus on being America's doctor because it's where his momentum would lie. When their doctor wouldn't take the time to talk to them, Oz had a magical way of explaining very complicated issues. He used little science experiments. He created videos. He was relatable, and he cared. That was his strength.

He'd had plenty of momentum in his life. The first time I met with him, my eyes instantly went to his mantel, where the Emmys were stacked pretty deep. I think every celebrity imaginable has gone on Dr. Oz's show—and remember, he got his TV start by being the resident doctor on *The Oprah Winfrey Show.* Oprah saw how much her viewers gave him their trust.

I became friends with Oz, and the more I got to know him, the more I appreciated his intellectual curiosity. So when I started writing about momentum, I wanted to talk to him because he's the master of explaining things. I was interested in what he'd have to say about achieving personal momentum since that's what his show is all about. When I sat down in Oz's office and began telling him about the book, he immediately sketched out a simple diagram [below].

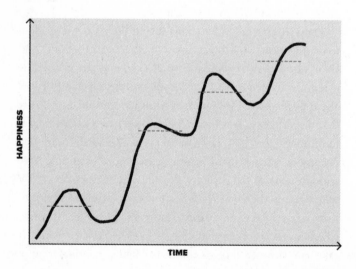

Pointing to the vertical line, he said, "This line is called HAPPY." And, he said, "This horizontal line across the bottom is called TIME." Happiness plotted against time. It was an intriguing idea.

Tracing his finger along the upward curve, he described the way people's lives go. They start to rise, and their best days are ahead of them, and they have momentum. They reach a point of happiness. But then happiness begins to decline, and they don't see their best days ahead anymore. When they see their satisfaction going down, they jump off their path and try to change course. But it often doesn't work.

Pointing to a place lower on the happiness curve, he explained that if you want to keep your personal momentum, with your best days ahead, you have to jump off earlier while you're still rising. You can't wait until you feel that your best days are behind you. When you're rising, you have the best optionality—the most choices and the most optimistic point of view. You have the most room to grow and the most space for momentum.

Oz explained that people often wait too long to make changes that generate momentum. They get stuck in ruts and routines. They get complacent. Everything is going well, and they don't think about the possibility that it could change. And then, boom!—they hit a wall and try to change course when they're at their weakest point. And they're not equipped for the change.

Obviously, unexpected events can happen at any point in life, but Oz's model is a good one for those who want to have an ongoing perspective of personal momentum. I grasped Oz's point immediately because, as someone who's always looking for momentum, I've had that restless energy throughout my life. Complacency—which is another way of saying stagnation—is a foreign concept to me. I firmly believe that happiness and momentum go hand in hand. You can't have happiness without momentum.

Think about it. Do you know anybody happy with their best days behind them?

Personal momentum starts with the decision that your best days are ahead of you, not behind you. This is a choice you can make about your life, regardless of your age, physical condition, professional status, or other factors. For example, consider how transformational it is to say at ages fifty or sixty, "My best days are ahead." This simple declaration changes the entire focus of your life. It projects optimism and produces movement.

I believe we are in a new era of personal momentum. One example of that is the body positivity movement. Body positivity shakes people loose from assumptions about their worth and capabilities based on the way they look. The shame around body image has permeated our culture for a long time, especially around weight. It's taken until now for a movement in body positivity to gain momentum, as people—usually women—are saying they're not going to take it anymore. Most women surveyed report that they feel pressured and demeaned by unrealistic standards of beauty, which are heightened by social media. They feel fat-shamed, even when they aren't overweight by objective measures. That's an old story. What's new is they're fighting back, and they're coming out of the closet to do it. The prevalence of plus-size models and the publication ban on airbrushing have been early signs of momentum.

The founders of the Body Positivity Institute have said that social media has been something of a double-edged sword. On the one hand, it has allowed for a mass of bullying and fat-shaming. But on the positive side, it has also engineered a movement for self-acceptance and empowered people to speak up.

When the actress Lena Dunham first appeared in the HBO series *Girls*, she stood out for flaunting her imperfect body, even in sex scenes. Her refusal to be ashamed of her body has made her a champion of the body positivity movement. In the spring of 2019, she posted a nude sunbathing photo on Instagram (covering up parts that might get it banned) with the message, "Any negativity that comes your way is just an excuse to love yourself even more, right? Comment below with a reason you love yourself. I'll go first: I'm a sober accountable adult who still loves to get naked."

It should surprise no one that the body positivity movement has received its share of blowback, usually in the form of thinly described contempt. Numerous articles and social media posts have accused it of supporting unhealthy lifestyles. The reasoning goes, if you don't judge people for being overweight, how are they ever going to have the motivation to eat more healthfully? In this context, shame is an acceptable motivation for change. Except shame doesn't produce change, only misery. Researchers have found that fear- and anxiety-based messages do not help people make better lifestyle choices. Positive messages do. In that respect, body positivity is actually a motivator for change, not an invitation to complacency. In the polarity between body perfection and body positivity, body perfection is stagnant, and body positivity has momentum.

PERSONAL MOMENTUM AS A BRAND

Social media has also capitalized on the idea of personal branding. If being loyal to a brand is important to its momentum, being faithful to *your* brand is important to personal momentum. Few people have captured the idea of the personal brand as completely as Kim Kardashian.

I'd hardly characterize myself as a Kardashian fan. Most of her followers are teenage girls and young women. But I have to admire the sweep of her influence. Kardashian has built an aura around herself for all of her millions of fans, where she is the voice they listen to. She is the ultimate influencer. She knows something they don't know, and she's going to tell them. She posts a picture or pitches a product or sends out a lifestyle tip, and across the world, you can almost hear the collective beep of texts popping off screens. Her critics say she's only famous for being famous—suggesting she's done nothing of worth to earn her widespread appeal. That's an elitist and meaningless view, which sounds envious. Everything she touches gets branded with that unique Kardashian stamp. She is masterful at curating her image. Her fame has even led to her being the frontwoman for compelling issues like gun control and unfair incarceration, and given her a platform for her personal struggle with infertility. So, how did she get so big?

Kardashian first created mass from her sex tape. That got her on people's radar. Sex tapes are good ways to build quick mass—that's just a fact, not a judgment. At the time, she was only marginally famous for being a pal of Paris Hilton. The sex tape jump-started Kardashian's fame, and she ran with it. She flaunted her curvy body and her impeccably contoured face and hair, and people were fascinated.

In 2007, Kardashian and her family secured a reality TV show, *Keeping Up with the Kardashians*, which became one of the most popular and durable reality shows of all time. They used it to build the Kardashian brand and boost the fortunes of other members of the family. But Kim Kardashian has always been the true star, the sun around whom lesser Kardashian planets revolve.

Since TV can only take you so far, Kardashian's momentum exploded with the rise of social media. It became her sweet spot. She is widely recognized as the "Queen of Social Media," with 224 million followers (and counting) across several platforms. Instagram is the Kardashian playground; she has 145 million followers and lucrative sponsorship deals. A single Kardashian product post on Instagram can earn her as much as half a million dollars. She has monetized momentum in ways that are out of the reach of mere mortals. Piggybacking off her older sister's success, the younger Kylie Jenner has grabbed momentum by becoming a huge media presence—and a billionaire.

Here's an example of Kardashian's supremacy. In 2016, while visiting Paris, robbers broke into her apartment and bound and gagged her. She thought they were going to kill her. It was a terrifying episode, and in the immediate aftermath, she completely closed down her social media accounts. She went "dark" for three months. But when she returned, posting a photo of her family on Instagram and Twitter, she was more popular than ever. Since momentum thrives on continuity, dropping out of sight would usually be the kiss of death. Not for Kardashian. It actually increased her momentum, driving her fans to want her more.

Kardashian's ability to be provocative is a big part of her appeal. Her marriage to Kanye West, an avid Trump fan, her nearly nude social media posts, and the ongoing family dramas have given her continued velocity. A famously dramatic cover photo in *Paper* magazine, with Kardashian's physical attributes on full display, was titled in a way that says it all: "Break the Internet."

KARDASHIAN METRICS

POLARIZATION: Love her or hate her, people obsess about her and follow her to see what she'll do or say next.

INNOVATION: Kardashian regularly goes through major face and body transformations, keeping her followers guessing about the next iteration. She never stops changing.

STICKY ISSUE: She's the very definition of sticky! It's not just that her mass of followers is huge. It's her ability to make people care about every detail of her life.

DISRUPTIVE: Unlike typical celebrities who are overprotective of their images, Kardashian lets followers deep inside her life, exposing her struggles and her failings.

IMPACT: Kardashian regularly transcends the narrative that she's shallow by getting involved in big issues, such as criminal justice reform. Now she's announced she's going to law school. She constantly reinvents and has an impact.

I've often thought that there were similarities between Kim Kardashian and Donald Trump. Like Trump, Kardashian has her share of haters. But whether people tune in to adore her or mock her, the point is that they're tuning in. Trump and Kardashian share a certain narcissism that dissolves the barriers to shameless self-promotion. Both gleefully make themselves look bad, continually raising the stakes.

Dr. Amanda Scheiner McClain, author of *Keeping Up the Kardashian Brand: Celebrity, Materialism, and Sexuality*, has observed that Kardashian and Trump are cut from the same mold: "Political views aside, the rise of the Kardashians and Trump is similar. They both started out rich and low-level celebrities; they both used reality TV to raise their national profile; they both use social media's direct connection to fans and the ability to construct and convey perceived authenticity to build a brand; both rode cultural trends of narcissism and materialism to high levels of celebrity."

EVERYTHING OLD IS NEW AGAIN

We often think of momentum as a brand-new and shiny thing, but the fashion industry teaches us that everything old can be new again. The fashion industry is a model of constant change, adapting to personal styles with ease, creating momentum in each cycle. Fashion "trends" are not so much trends as they are modifications of previous styles. And today's market arena is no longer chained to the fashion magazines that dominated style for decades. It's out in the universe, with fashion bloggers and social media dominating consumer shopping habits.

A fascinating aspect of this movement is recycling, a rapidly dominating fashion industry worth upwards of $2.4 trillion. People are not just buying old clothes; they are buying and wearing the evolved and remodeled versions created to conform to the new style modes.

For me, this is a fascinating example of disruption, not only in an industry, but in a personal movement. Consumers are literally reevaluating personal style in a way that is dynamic and ever-changing, without being beholden to the old rules of fashion.

YOUR PERSONAL MOMENTUM

Is your personal "brand" soaring or slumping? What does it mean to achieve maximum momentum in your life?

We usually think of momentum in its application to politics, business, movements, and even sports. But what about the YOU-brand? How do you become a momentum master in your own life?

Let's look at how you can take the metrics for momentum and apply them personally:

Polarization: In your personal life, polarization simply means, "I choose." One style over another. One philosophy over another. One way of being that is separate and unique from others.

Innovation: The ability to keep changing and growing. Innovation in your life means not getting stuck in a rut—taking risks and exploring new opportunities.

Stickiness: What's your label—the thing that defines you?

Disruption: How willing are you to pursue a completely unexpected course?

Impact: Does your life have a higher purpose than just yourself? Are you engaged in being part of a change? Do you spend your emotional and material capital on making a difference?

WHAT MAKES YOU TICK?

In my first book, *What Makes You Tick: How Successful People Do It and What You Can Learn from Them*, I interviewed captains of industry in business, politics, sports, and entertainment. I wanted to quantify the successful personality, and I devoted a whole section to Natural Born Leaders. I identified their inner-personality traits:

- Self-confidence
- Big-picture thinking
- Take-charge personality
- Inspirational/motivational spirit
- Helpful approach
- Comfortable delegating

Leaders inspire us, but not everyone is cut out to be a leader. However, everyone can be aspirational in their own life, and that means seeking momentum. If you don't have momentum, you can't innovate, you can't be successful, and you can't be happy. Without momentum, your life is stuck. Everybody wants to be with somebody who has momentum and is relevant. They don't want to be with somebody who is standing still or stuck in the past.

Momentum is always thinking about the future. If you have momentum, you always know that your best days are ahead.

CHAPTER NINE

TAKE THE
MOMENTUM CHALLENGE

You've made it to the end of *Maximum Momentum*. This book is designed to give you the inside scoop on how successful people, companies, and movements fuel their momentum, and inspire you to think about momentum in your own life—personally, in relationships, for your company or brand, or for the causes you believe in.

The Momentum Challenge is a jumping-off point for that inspiration. Do you have momentum? If yes, how do you sustain it? If no, how do you get it back? These questions are meant to help predict where your momentum is today and motivate you to take the actions to get it and keep it.

1. Are your best days ahead or behind?
   a. Best days ahead
   b. Best days behind
   c. Split/somewhere in the middle

The "best days" question is the key to momentum. It's about optimism, being future-focused, having a vision, and knowing where you're headed. When a brand's best days are ahead, it's because its consumers are excited about what is to come and believe in the brand's ability to evolve—to adapt and change with the time to better meet their needs and to stay ahead. If people believe the best days are behind, a drastic change is needed to rebound. When the answer is a split, it's because consumers don't know. And that is death. Uncertainty. Some consumers have hope, others have given up. No-man's-land.

The same is true in your personal life. When you view your best days as ahead, everything is possible. The road is open for movement. There's exhilaration in living a life of possibility.

LESSON: Best days ahead is about the **future**. Having a vision and inspiring those around that vision is key to momentum. Best days behind signals defeat. If you're not sure or stuck in the middle, you need to shake loose to build momentum.

2. Where are you on the Momentum Curve?

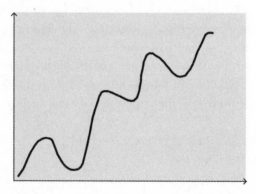

a. On the rise.
b. At the peak.
c. Starting to decline.

We learned from Dr. Oz that when you are at your peak, it may be too late to change your momentum. The best time to get momentum is when you have momentum—you're on the rise and moving. It's easiest to adapt, evolve, and change course when you're on the rise and in a position of strength.

There are countless examples of brands that have prospered with this theory. For example, Gin Lane was a super-cool agency, the designer of many hot startups with momentum—such as Warby Parker and Allbirds. As it was on the rise, it pivoted to Pattern Brands and developed a new kind of company. It capitalized on its momentum to change.

In your personal life or even in your career, if you are at the peak of success and happiness, you're already beginning to stall. To stay fresh and future-oriented, and keep your personal momentum going, seek change while you're growing. It's harder to change course when reaching the peak feels so close and attainable, but there are always more mountains to climb.

LESSON: When you are at the top, the only way to go is down. You still have something to stand on, but it could quickly be gone before you get a chance to act. And when you are starting from the decline, desperation and the extent of the challenge will make a climb back much more challenging. Make a move to maximize your momentum when you are still on the ascent; don't wait for your peak—it won't last.

3. Are you creating FOMO (fear of missing out)? Do people want to be a part of your orbit?
   a. Yes.
   b. Want to but don't know how.
   c. No.

When you create FOMO, it means that people want to be a part of what you are all about.

They feel that they are missing out if they aren't part of what you're creating. You have social currency—relevancy. You are fueling the modern-day watercooler talk (tweeting, sharing, engaging). What you're offering is something they can't get from anywhere else. It's a badge, an unspoken symbol of your influence.

You can translate the idea of having FOMO to your personal life. You can make an impact within your social circle, influencing those closest to you.

LESSON: Everyone wants to make a difference in the world in big and small ways. Creating FOMO is another measure of how you achieve this.

4. Are you willing to be polarizing?
   a. Your point of view is an affront to some people but deeply resonates with others.
   b. Your point of view resonates with some people but doesn't totally alienate others.
   c. You try to appease both sides.

As Alexander Hamilton put it, "Those who stand for nothing, fall for anything."

Taking a stand is a form of polarization, and polarization creates energy. It gets people's attention and gives them something to rally around. Polarization makes you interesting, makes you stand out, and makes people want to learn more. We know, for example, that the most memorable advertising—such as Nike's Colin Kaepernick ad—gets people talking. The same reality applies personally. When your position turns some people off, it can make you more attractive to others. A study from OK Cupid determined that people with more polarizing profile pics (based on ratings) were more likely to get messages.

LESSON: Take a stand on something you believe in, even if it pisses off some people. It will reap you more rewards.

    5. Are you on the move?
        a. Do you look ahead and plan how you will change to get there?
        b. Do you wait and see how things develop?
        c. Are you satisfied with the status quo?

It's easiest to stick with the status quo, assuming that what worked in the past will continue to work. It's even easier to be reactive to what comes your way. Lingering in the present can feel like a safe place to be. It's hard to look out into the future and make a bet on what comes next. It takes courage. But the status quo is offering a false sense of security because change *will* come, whether you want it or not. It's much better to drive your own momentum than to let it happen to you.

LESSON: Complacency and stagnation are enemies. Have the courage and confidence to bet on yourself!

YOUR MOMENTUM PLAN

Evaluate your responses to the five momentum questions.

If most or all of your answers are (a.), you have great momentum potential, and you probably already experience momentum in your life. Just remember that momentum requires constant transformation. The question for you is, "What's next?"

Ask yourself each morning, "What is the action I am going to take to increase my momentum today?" Think of it as your momentum ritual, a habit that gets incorporated into the way you think about your day.

If most or all of your answers are (b.), you need to move quickly to avoid stagnation.

Standing still is a dangerous place to be if your goal is momentum. You need a plan. What is your weakness when it comes to creating momentum? Are you nervous about controversy? Are you overly protective of what you already have? Are you afraid that bold action will not pay off?

Start to get in the momentum mindset by taking small steps. What is one change you can make each week that will begin to develop a momentum habit? What is the small risk you can take in your professional or personal life that will get you started? Remember, change will come whether you are seeking it or not. Decide that you're going to control your destiny and your momentum.

If most or all of your answers are (c.), you're in a momentum crisis. You're stuck. Think about it. How did you get there? Was there a time when you had momentum? How did you lose it? What choices did you make that diluted your impact? What story did you tell yourself about taking risks that paralyzed your performance?

As you strive to regain momentum in your life, who are the role models you can turn to for inspiration and guidance? Look for examples of those who turned failure into success, and consider how you can learn from their example.

The most important thing to know about momentum is that it is completely under your control. No one can give you momentum, and no one can take it away. It's up to you to create a life where your best days are always ahead of you.

ABOUT THE AUTHOR

Mike Berland is the founder and CEO of Decode_M, a research and analytics firm that decodes data into momentum for its clients.

He has represented prominent political figures, major companies, and social movements throughout his career including Airbnb, Lyft, Nike, Microsoft, Facebook, Estée Lauder Companies, the National Hockey League, Major League Baseball, Shell, CVS, Samsung, Unilever, Coca-Cola, and Michael Bloomberg.

Named "The Genius Pollster" by MSNBC, Berland is also the best-selling author of *Fat-Burning Machine*, a two-time New York City Marathon finisher, and a three-time Ironman World Championships Kona, Hawaii finisher.